Catalogue of the Sardinian, Etruscan and Italic Bronze statuettes in the Danish National Museum

Helle Salskov Roberts

Aarhus University Press

CATALOGUE OF THE SARDINIAN, ETRUSCAN AND ITALIC BRONZE STATUETTES IN THE DANISH NATIONAL MUSEUM

GÖSTA ENBOM MONOGRAPHS

General editor:
Bodil Bundgaard Rasmussen

Editorial board:
Mark L. Lawall, John Lund,
Dyfri Williams

Gösta Enbom Monographs is
a peer reviewed series

Published with support from:
Dronning Margrethes og
Prins Henriks Fond
Landsdommer V. Gieses Legat
VELUX FONDEN

Graphic design:
Nina Grut, MDD

Printed at Narayana Press

Typeset with Stone Serif
and Stone Sans

ISBN 978 87 7219 454 7
ISSN 1904-6219

Aarhus University Press
Langelandsgade 177
DK-8200 Aarhus N
unipress.dk

International distributors:
oxbow.co.uk
isd.com

All catalogue photos:
National Museum of Denmark.

Front cover:
Standing woman with diadem,
Danish National Museum
inv. 4203. Cat. 56.

Back cover:
Standing woman with tall
headdress, Danish National
Museum inv. 116. Cat. 54.

Athlete, Danish National
Museum inv. ABa 707. Cat. 42.

Amphora attributed to the painter Syriskos, Athens 500-470 BC, Collection of Classical and Near Eastern Antiquities, The National Museum of Denmark, i.n. Chr. VIII 320.

Nationalmuseet
National Museum of Denmark

MIX
Paper from
responsible sources
FSC® C010651

Table of Contents

Preface

BY HELLE SALSKOV ROBERTS

I am pleased to be able to present the collection of Sardinian, Etruscan and Italic bronze statuettes of the Danish National Museum in the Department of Ancient Cultures of Denmark and the Mediterranean, of which only some of the more spectacular examples have been published. It is, however, my hope that many of the other pieces may contribute to the understanding of important aspects of the varied cultures that flourished on the Italian Mainland and on one of the major islands of the western Mediterranean for many centuries before the Roman conquest.

I am grateful to the Head of Research and Collections Bodil Bundgaard Rasmussen and to Senior Researcher John Lund for facilitating my work with these objects and for their support and fruitful discussions. I also want to thank Nora M. Petersen for daily assistance in the library. During my work with the bronze statuettes I have received much help from the staff of the Department of Greek and Roman Antiquities in the British Museum as well as from the Ashmolean Museum in Oxford and the Scottish National Museum in Edinburgh. I am also grateful for having been allowed access to the collections of Antiquités grecques et romaines du Louvre, Le Musée d'Archéologie National de Saint-Germain-en-Laye, the Archeologiccal Museum in Florence, the Villa Giulia Museum in Rome and the Vatican, as well as many provincial museums in Italy.

I have been fortunate enough to enjoy several periods of study at the Danish Academy in Rome and I have also had the privilege of using the library of the neighbouring Swedish Institute, for which I extend my sincere thanks.

For great assistance with the electronic media I want to thank my friend Jane Halberg and last, but not least, I am deeply obliged to my husband John Roberts for his constant patience and support.

Finally, I wish to express my gratitude to Dronning Margrethes og Prins Henriks Fond, to Landsdommer V. Gieses Legat and to the Velux Foundation for their generous support of the publication of this catalogue.

Introduction

HISTORY OF THE COLLECTION

The beginnings of the collection of Greek and Roman antiquities in Denmark have been traced by H. C. Bering Liisberg in *"Kunstkammeret. Dets stiftelse og Ældste Historie"*, Copenhagen 1897. Many of the Danish Kings have been patrons of art and the results of their activities as collectors can be seen in the various departments of the Danish National Museum. Antique bronzes were one of the fields of interest and some pieces are known to have been in the Royal Collection before 1737, the earliest date recorded in the inventories, and were, perhaps, originally acquired much earlier.

In the Eighteenth Century the influential politician and Minister Ove Høegh-Guldberg, who died in 1808, had been a passionate collector, especially of antique figurines, and after his death the King acquired his collection (*Antik-Cabinettet, 1851*, 43 ff.).

The King who had a specific interest in classical antiquity was Christian VIII. In his youth he travelled in Italy during the years 1819-20 and made many valuable contacts who helped him in building a fine collection of antiquities which, following his death in 1848, was incorporated into the Antik-Cabinet in 1851. This became part of the Danish National Museum when it was officially founded in 1892.

The history of the Royal collection in general is related by Victor Hermansen in the above- mentioned *Antik-Cabinettet 1851* and, in the same work, Niels Breitenstein, former Keeper of the Department of Oriental and Classical Antiquities, – as the Department was then called – made a detailed study of the acquisition of the vases in the King's collection. Much of the correspondence between the King and his various contacts also mentions bronzes that may have been acquired along with vases. This, for instance, was the case with the acquisition of the important vase collection belonging to Capecelatro, the Archbishop of Taranto (*op.cit.* p. 62 ff.). With the vases came about one hundred bronzes, most of which were not of artistic merit, as pointed out by the King's adviser P. O. Brønsted. Most of figurines are very crude specimens of Herakles, presumably Umbrian and Central Italian local products (ABa 225-232, Cat 117; 95; 108; 111; 118; 10; 88; 104, and ABa 234-235, Cat.121; 123).

The acquisition of the Archbishop's collection was accomplished through the good offices of the Danish archaeologist P. O. Brøndsted (1780-1842), who travelled extensively in Greece and Italy and lived for many years in Rome. He was the archaeological adviser and agent of the Danish Crown Prince Christian Frederik, later King Christian VIII, whose interest in classical archaeology provided the base for the development of the collection of Near Eastern and Classical Antiquities of the Danish National Museum. The Prince travelled himself in Italy in the years 1819-20 and met the Archbishop. Antique bronzes were also provided for the collection in the years 1856-57. These pieces are likely to be of Italian origin.

The letters **AB** in front of the inventory numbers are found on all objects entered into the inventory of 1825 as Greek or Roman. The addition of the letter **a** indicates that the object is of metal and is therefore used for all the bronzes. This inventory system for the collection was made by Bishop Frederik Münter and the Professor of Philology, Børge Thorlacius, who were given the task of incorporationg it into the Royal Art Museum (*Antik-Cabinettet*, p. 49). From 1839 Christian Jürgensen Thomsen was Keeper of this museum, which, after the death of the King Christian VIII in 1848, was enriched by his collection in 1851. C. J. Thomsen's major rearrangement of the collection was based on a chronological principle. In 1846 he travelled extensively in Italy and Germany buying, *inter alia*, many bronze objects for the Museum.

Many Danish artists and learned men travelled in Europe in the middle of the Nineteenth Century and some brought back various antique statuettes or utensils, which were often subsequently offered to the Antik-Cabinet. The greatest private collector of this kind was the sculptor Bertel Thorvaldsen, who, during his long stay in Rome, had acquired many antiques, which, however, at his death in 1844, became part of the Thorvaldsen Museum. Many of the bronze figurines and other antique objects are of the same type as those belonging to the Danish National Museum, but unfortunately Thorvaldsen was not in the habit of making notes on the sources of his collection.

Artists whose collections eventually came into the possession of the Antik-Cabinet include the landscape painter Thorvald Læssøe and the sculptors H. Freund and Chr. Freund, who all worked in Italy.

In 1854-55 C. F. Herbst (1818-1911) and the Prehistoric archaeologist J. J. A. Worsaae (1821-85) visited Rome, Naples and Pavia.

After 1865-66 the cataloguing system of 1825, which had capital letters followed by a letter denoting the material, was abandoned, no doubt because of C. J. Thomsen's principle that a chronological order was more important than an arrangement according to material. In 1866 the name Antik-Cabinet was changed to "The Royal Collection of Antiquities", and objects acquired after that date were given simple consecutive numbers, a system that prevails today.

From 1866 Ludvig Müller was Director of the new museum and he enlarged the collection of bronzes by buying on the international art market, often at sales in Paris, his main contact being the firm of Rollin et Feuardent. Among his early purchases are some good Etruscan pieces, such as the archaic dancing satyr (Inv. no. 93 **Cat. 44**) and the Etruscan kore wearing a tutulus (Inv. no. 116, **Cat. 54**).

In 1871 Ludvig Müller went to Italy and bought some Etruscan pieces from Professor Biondelli in Milan, with whom the museum had previously been in contact. These included a warrior statuette (Inv. no. 516, **Cat. 9**).

A number of objects were acquired in Paris. These include an Etruscan female statuette (Inv. no. 946, **Cat. 55**).

In 1879 the collection was enriched by the bequest of a large number of bronzes, mainly Etruscan, which had been bought in Rome in 1876 by August Willads Bech, the owner of Valbygaard.

Following Mr. Bech's death in 1877 his widow handed over his collection, which had previously belonged to the Roman art dealer Basseggio and who is known to have obtained most of his bronzes from the Vulci excavations (Sotheby Sale Catalogue 13th July, 1838). From this bequest are the club-brandishing Herakles types (Inv. no. 1250c, e, f, g, h, i, **Cat. 98; 110; 96; 97; 101**), and other Herakles types such as Inv. no. 1250 b and d (**Cat. 124; 109**). The bequest also comprised a large number of schematic idols (Inv. no. 1248, **Cat. 29** (male) and 1249, **Cat. 39**, (female), of types mainly found in the Central Apennine region.

At the sale of the Gréau Collection in Paris in June 1885 the Museum acquired an Etruscan animal figurine (Inv. no. 2289, **Cat. 134**) with a very fine smooth greyish-green patina.

From the January 1886 catalogue of Sambon, Florence, were bought two votive objects, one in the shape of an arm and another in the shape of a leg (inv. nos. 3094-95, **Cat. 129-130**).

In 1891 Chr. Blinkenberg bought from private collectors in Rome two statuettes of Herakles brandishing the club (Inv. no. 3762, **Cat. 89** and Inv. no.3763, **Cat. 93**).

In 1894 the painter Simonetti sold the large, solid-cast female statuette (Inv. no. 4203, **Cat. 56**), which was said to have been found in Romagna and which came from the Collection of Count Ruffo di Rimini. On the same occasion was bought a Tinia of the "Hellenistic ruler" type (Inv. no. 4752, **Cat. 48**), said to have been found in the Tiber.

In 1897 the Museum received the gift of a number of crude votive statuettes, bought by a private collector in Rome, including warriors in cut-out sheet bronze) Inv. no.4787-89, **Cat. 27-28**) and female idols in long dress (Inv. no. 4790-96, **Cat. 31-35; 40-41**), both types being especially common in finds from the Central Apennine region.

From Pacini in Florence Blinkenberg bought two male statuettes in Archaic style and likely to have been produced in Northwest Etruria (inv. nos. 4807-4808, **Cat. 3-4**). According to the dealer's information they were found in a tomb in the Spring of 1898 at Castello, 3 km outside the Porta S. Gallo, Florence, with two similar statuettes, which were sold to the Archeological Museum in Florence.

Later additions to the Collection in the Nineteenth and Twentieth Centuries were mainly bought from or donated by private collectors, usually without information on provenance.

Catalogue

Sardinian, Etruscan and Italic Statuettes

Sardinian

CAT. 1. STANDING WOMAN

Inv. no. 5367.
H.: 20,4 cm.
Provenance: Said to be from Le Marche.
Acquisition: Bought in Rome in 1902-3 from A. Simonetti. Formerly in Collection Blacker, Paris, with the provenance given as Rome.
Bibliography: Reinach III, 267,8. RM 1928, 77 note 99. Guido 1963, 174 ff.; 268; pl. 49. National Museum Guide 1968, ill. p. 72; 73. Lilliu 1966 no. 80. Dietz 1981, 222-236, esp. 233 f., ill.226 f. Jürgeit 1983, 121, figs. 4-5 in Antidoron Jürgen Thimme, 119-124. Danish National Museum Guide 1994, 125.
Technique: Solid cast. Under heels lump from casting, used for fixing the statuette. Cleaned mechanically in 1980 when a large lump by the right arm was removed. Surface now fairly even and matt. Dark blue and green patina with lighter green patches. Missing: left hand.

Metal composition:	Cu	Sn	Zn	Pb	Fe	Ni	Mn
	87.9	11.7	0.01	0.03	0.2	0.05	-

Cu, Sn, Zn found by atomic absorbtion method, the other components by semiquantitative analysis.

Woman standing frontally on both feet, right hand raised over shoulder, palm forward. Left arm extended at level of waist, hand missing. Dressed in various garments, the innermost having long sleeves and reaching the feet. Its lower part covered by vertical grooves, possibly indicating folds of a thin material. The same stylization is seen at the sleeve-end over the right wrist. Over this are layers of garment of varying length, made from a smooth material without folds. The rounded U-shaped neckline of one of them, the innermost (?), appears over the outer garment, which is draped over the left shoulder and disappears in a slightly curved line under the right arm. This outer garment is finished at knee-level by a fringe, presumably the warp-ends of a woollen material. It looks different from the fold of the innermost garment, which is also at a level different from that of the next layer of material. Finally she wears a large cloak over the shoulders. It is folded double at the back to about knee-level. The single part is decorated at the back by horizontal lines. The sides of the cloak have fringes shown by oblique strokes. The bottom line of the cloak has seven, originally eight, oval pendents, which might be the warp-ends of the material tied together. The figure wears a conical hat with a broad rim, the thickened edge of which is slightly turned upwards. The top-side of the hat is decorated with two concentric circles of oblique strokes. Under the hat she has a veil, which hangs down the sides of the neck and is tucked under the cloak and disappears under the neckline of the inner garment.

The hair, showing only over the forehead, has a central parting. The forehead is very low and the eyebrows form a continous plastic notched ridge. The eyes are large and bulging, not quite symmetrical, the right one being fairly square and obliquely set. The nose is large and prominent, the mouth small with unsmiling vaguely defined lips. Small, firm chin; the shape of the head is long and square, the neck very long, the body plank-like with very small breasts. The fingers of the hand and the toes of the feet extremely long, indicated by deep grooves.

Cf for large hat Lilliu 1966 no. 79; no. 81 = Thimme 1980, 144, both from Terralba, Western Sardinia. The large cloak is worn by more statuettes, Lilliu 1966 no.75 = Thimme 1980 no. 136; Lilliu 1966 no. 76 = Thimme 1980, no. 137; 138; 139; Lilliu 1966 no. 123 = Thimme 1980 no. 140 the last from S. Vittoria, Serri; Taramelli 1913,97 fig. 2. = Lilliu 1966 no. 69, from Nuragus, Central Sardinia.

Comment

The diagonal draping of the outer garment is found on several of these statuettes, and on some it appears that this garment is wrapped round the body, one side being open like a Greek peplos, *eg* Thimme 1980 nos. 136; 137; 138.

Most of the parallels stand in the same position, the right hand raised with palm forward and the left extended, holding a pyxis or plate with various offerings, thus pointing to an interpretation as worshippers or priestesses. Most finds are without provenance, but the well sanctuary at Serri on the plateau of Central Sardinia has brought forward one female statuette as well as several figurines of warriors and animals. At Nuragus, north of Serri, another cloaked woman was found in an ancient well. The two statuettes with large hats are said to have come from Terralba in the Western part of the island. The Danish National Museum specimen is one of the largest female statuette, the one from Nuragus reaching 18 cms, but most being 13-14 cm. The chronology of Sardinian bronze statuettes is not well established. Sardinia has obviously

Cat. 1. Ca. 1:1.

had a bronze working production reaching back into the Bronze Age, with far reaching contacts to the Near East. The finds from the sanctuary at Serri show a suggested range from the Eighth to the Sixth Centuries. The products have pronounced local character that does not easily fit into other better-known figural traditions. Finds from the Italian Mainland are not helpful for female statuettes, the only statuette, from the Vulcian Bartoccini tomb of the late Ninth Century BC, being that of a warrior in a rather different style.

In view of the find of a nuragic bronze boat found at Capo Colonna in the sanctuary of Hera Lacinia, now in the archaeological Museum of Crotone, (Spadea 1996, p. 22 no. 33, figs. 27-29), the provenance for the Copenhagen statuette given as "Le Marche" by the dealer gains a little more credibility than has sometimes been given to it.

Seventh Century BC or later?

Ad Cat. no. 1:

Jürgeit 1983 discusses in detail the clothing of the Sardinian statuettes.

After cleaning, it is possible to study the details of the Copenhagen statuette more clearly and get a better understanding of the clothing. The outer garment should most likely be understood as a rectangular piece of woollen cloth folded double from over the breasts to the knees, where the warp-ends form a fringe. The material covers the left shoulder and passes under the right arm-pit. Jürgeit refers to other statuettes where the open sides of the cloth can be seen on the left side of the wearer. Under the outer garment, the Copenhagen statuette has a long plain tunic with a rounded U-shaped neckline and long sleeves finished off with a smooth border. At the wrist and over the ankles appears the innermost garment, with closely-set vertical grooves likely rendering the crinkly folds of a thin material. These grooves are at a level different from the plain borderline above and thus not likely to represent a fringe of this. The large cloak is folded double from the shoulders to about the knees, with the wheft-ends forming fringes along the sides.

The seven, originally eight, oval lumps at the lower border could be the warp-ends tied together in knots. Jürgeit 1983, 122 suggests that the cloak could be made of skins worn with the furside inwards and decorated with patterns on the outside. There is no indication of fur on the smooth inside of the cloak of the Copenhagen statuette, where the fringes are mostly compatible with a woollen cloth. The measurements of a life-size cloak would be about 2,50 m - 3 m .

The short cloak of the Copenhagen male figure Cat. 2 with the lengthwise mid-rib might rather be understood as leather, but there are also examples of this cloak with a border fringe, *eg* Thimme 1980, 287 no. 114.A.

Cat. 1. Ca 1:1.

CAT. 2. STANDING MAN

Inv. no. 5366
H.: 16,8 cm.
Provenance: Unknown.
Acquisition: 1907. Bought from Rollin et Feuardent, Paris.
Bibliography: Lilliu 1966 no.53. Guido 1963, pl. 48. Danish National Museum Guide 1968, 72. Coles/Harding 1979, pl. 232 c. Dietz 1981, 222-236, esp. 223-225, illus. 224 f.
Technique: Solid cast. Surface smooth with a few corroded areas. Olive-green patina with a few verdigris spots. Missing: Left hand and both feet from above ankles.

Metal composition:	Cu	Sn	Zn	Pb	Fe	Ni	Mn
	92.9	7.2	0.01	-	-	0.03	-

Cu, Sn, Zn found by atomic absorbtion method, the other components by semiquantitative analysis.

Standing on both legs, feet apart, knees slightly bent. Right hand raised, palm forward. Left arm advanced, bent at elbow. He is wearing a garment wrapped round the body, twice, maybe three times, with one end covering the right shoulder and another part of the material coming over the left shoulder and passing diagonally under the right arm. Experiment shows that it takes a length of material of about 8 m. Over the left shoulder is a broad strap holding the dagger, of which the hilt is visible. On the head is an oval cap with thickened edge. Between the cap and ear there is a row of oblique strokes of descending length, which may be understood as either tassels hanging from the cap or as indication of a hairstyle. In the latter case the back of the head would be cleanshaven.

The head is long with a straight nose and eyebrows forming a single, plastic notched ridge. The eyeballs are rectangular, the outer end placed lower than the inner. Iris of the right eye indicated as a flat circle. The mouth is small with straight lips. The chin very small, neck and torso long, the limbs thin. Extremely long fingers indicated on the preserved hand.

The style is close to the large statuette Lilliu 1966 no.4 from the sanctuary of S. Vittoria, Serri, the finds of which cover the Eighth to Sixth Centuries BC.

The details of the cap with fringes (or hair?) are also found on the son held by mother, Lilliu 1966 no. 68.

Cf Cat.1. Thimme 1980 no.114.

Seventh Century BC or later?

Cat. 2. Ca 1:1.

Etruscan and Italic

MALE FIGURES

CAT. 3. STANDING MAN

Inv. no. 4808.
H.: 14,8 cm.
Provenance: Said to have been found in tomb at Castello, 3 km outside Porta S.Gallo, Florence, with Inv. no. 4807 and two similar statuettes, now in the Florence Archaeological Museum, Inv. nos. 77431-77432.
Acquisition: 1898. Bought in Florence from the dealer Pacini.
Bibliography: Riis 1941, 139, pl. 23,1. Laviosa 1959, *BdA* XLIV, 198 note 14. Richardson 1983, 109 no.3, pl. 52, fig. 197.
Technique: Solid cast. Matt surface. Olive-green patina. Three holes (casting faults) at left side of neck. Outer part of right foot broken off.

Bearded male, wearing perizoma wrapped round hips and overlapping at the front. Borders decorated with oblique strokes. He is standing frontally on both feet, arms stretched along sides. The hands are clenched, fingers indicated. Hair divided in the middle and falling down over neck and shoulders in a large mass, cut straight at the bottom. Fine lines indicate strands of hair. Low forehead, small, slightly aquiline nose, straight mouth. Prominent cheek bones. Ears free. Pointed beard, leaving front of chin free. Five lines on beard, oblique strokes on eye-brows. Breast vaguely modelled, kneecaps indicated. Spine drawn by deep furrow.

Cf Magi 1934, 413-418, pl. 45,1-2. For perizoma, Cf Laviosa 1959, 193-198. Camporeale 2009, 65, fig. 8. Cristofani 1985, 134 no. 21, from Castello (Florence inv. 77431). Santuari 1985,177 no. 10.2.9, votive deposit of Fonte Veneziana, Arezzo.

Comment

The Castello tomb contained four statuettes, two bearded kouroi with loincloth and two beardless nude kouroi. The Copenhagen statuette is not virtually a replica of Florence 77431, as stated by Richardson, but is, indeed, very close. The Florence specimen has a more prominent chin, and the hairline is different. Similarly, Cat. 4 (inv. 4807) is not a replica, but very close to Florence 77432, from which it, however, differs, especially in the facial details. The legs of the Florence statuette are joined to mid calves, whereas the legs of the Copenhagen figure are separated from mid thighs. All four statuettes were indubitably produced in the same workshop. The closeness and many analogies between the two statuettes from Castello tomb, now in Florence, and the Copenhagen statuettes are explained by the technique described by Formigli a propos of two statuettes in Arezzo, now ascribed to the deposit of Fonte Veneziana (Formigli 1984, 123 in Bocci Pacini 1984, 121, pl. I,a,b,c; pl. IV a). Formigli presumes that an initial negative mould provided with one or more valves was used. From this mould it was possible to extract the wax models, which could then be remodelled separately. Because of the casting faults the bronze caster may have wanted to make another copy. See also Formigli's description of the indirect lost wax casting technique in Cristofani 1985, 36-38, figs. 3-4. Magi, followed by Riis, places them in the third quarter of the 6th Century BC, whereas Cristofani and Richardson prefer a date around the middle of the 6th Century BC. The beard is similar to that of the Stockholm kouros (Richter 1960, no. 26 fig. 123-125). For perizoma, *cf* stone torso from Marciano, Camporeale 2009, 65, fig. 8.

See also Cat. 4. (inv. 4807).

Northwest Etruscan.
550-525 BC.

Cat. 3.

Cat. 3. Ca 1:1.

CAT. 4. STANDING NAKED MAN

Inv. no. 4807.
H.: 10,7 cm.
Provenance: Said to have been found in tomb at Castello, 3 km outside Porta S. Gallo, Florence together with Cat. 3 (Inv. no. 4808) and two similar statuettes, now in the Florence Archaeological Museum, inv. 77431-77432.
Acquisition: 1898. Bought in Florence from the dealer Pacini.
Bibliography: Riis 1941, 138, pl.23,2. Richardson 1983, 104 no. 4, pl. 52, fig. 198 (Early Archaic, Series B, group 2).
Technique: Solid cast. Rather corroded, matt surface. Pale green patina. Front part of both feet missing.

Cat. 4. Ca 1:1.

Naked, beardless male. Standing with legs joined to mid thigh, one slightly advanced. Arms held along sides, free of body around waist, hands pressed flat to mid thighs. Head very large. Low forehead, almond-shaped eyes, low arches. Small short nose. Broad mouth with full, protruding lips. Prominent chin. Square lower face. The hair, parted over forehead and hanging down over shoulders, cut off in a straight line, incised with vertical lines from top of crown. Broad, but sloping shoulder. No modelling of torso.

Cf Magi 1934, 413-418, pl. 45,2, to which this statuette is very close, but no replica. Richter 1960, no. 26, figs. 123-125 (Stockholm no. 314) Richardson 1983, pl. 57, figs. 209-211 (Ghiaccio Forte inv. 73,14, from Ghiaccio Forte).

Comment

The Stockholm kouros, sometimes thought to be Greek or South Italian, but more likely is Etruscan, and the Copenhagen statuette are obviously connected by stance, body structure and proportions. The head of the Copenhagen bronze shows, however, a very different style, with none of the ionizing features which appear in the Stockholm kouros. The bronze from Talamone, Florence inv. 73234 (Cristofani 1985, no. 22) and the Impruneta kouros, (Galli 1918, 211f., figs. 1-2) sometimes brought into the discussion, are not particularly close.

The feature of the hands pressed flat against the thighs is found in Etruscan bronzes from the earliest period, but in Greek marble kouroi it is extremely rare, the only clear example in Richter 1960 being her no. 27, fig. 126-128 (BM B 330) from Kamiros, of her Sounion Group. In representations of early female figures it is more common, *eg* the ivory statuettes from the Dipylon tomb (Richter 1968, figs. 16-22) and in the bronze found at the Acropolis (*eadem* 1968, figs. 23-24).

The closest parallel is the bronze from Ghiaccio Forte (Prov. of Grosseto), where a votive deposit was found during the American excavations in the 1970's (Del Chiaro 1973, 327 ff.). Del Chiaro, who refers to the Castello bronzes, dates the new statuette to the first half of the Sixth Century BC.

The stance and position of arms and hands of the Copenhagen bronze are found on the Monteleone chariot repoussé, which is dated by context to 550-530 BC. On balance, the Castello bronzes were most likely produced after the middle of the Sixth Century BC in a workshop in Northwestern Etruria.

Cf Cat. 3.

Northwest Etruscan.
550-525 BC.

CAT. 5. STANDING MAN. KOUROS TYPE
Inv. no. ABa 868.
H. with tang: 10,3 cm. Without tang: 8,5 cm.
Provenance: Unknown.
Acquisition: 1861. Bequeathed by Th. Reutze, Vienna.
Bibliography: Unpublished.
Technique: Olive-green patina, smooth surface. Tang under feet.

Naked kouros standing with left foot slightly advanced. Both arms free of body and stretched a little forward, with closed fists, the right slightly higher than the left. Broad shoulders, breast modelled; long, slim thighs joined at waist. Hair arranged in thick roll over forehead, hanging down nape of neck in short mass. Ears indicated outside hair. Small, prominent nose. No other facial features.

Cf Bieber 1915, pl. 38 no. 119. Richardson 1983, 117 no. 17 (Oxford 196/78 Fortnum B 21) from Malta; 123 no. 1, figs. 254-256 (Cortona 1702); 123 no. 2, fig. 257 (Florence 98); 131 no. 11, fig. 289 (BM 516).

Comment
The roundness of the body, as well as the hairstyle, connects this statuette with the kouroi statuettes from the votive deposit of Fonte Veneziana (Cristofani 1985, 88-91). The affinity of the Oxford Ashmolean statuette, also referred to here, to the Fonte Veneziana deposit has also been noted by Richardson, who suggests that it might be a stray from that workshop. The more detached position of the arms of the Copenhagen kouros points, however, to a period later than this deposit, and this very feature also shows affinity with the athlete type which is more frequent in Late Archaic material.

North Etruscan.
500-480 BC.

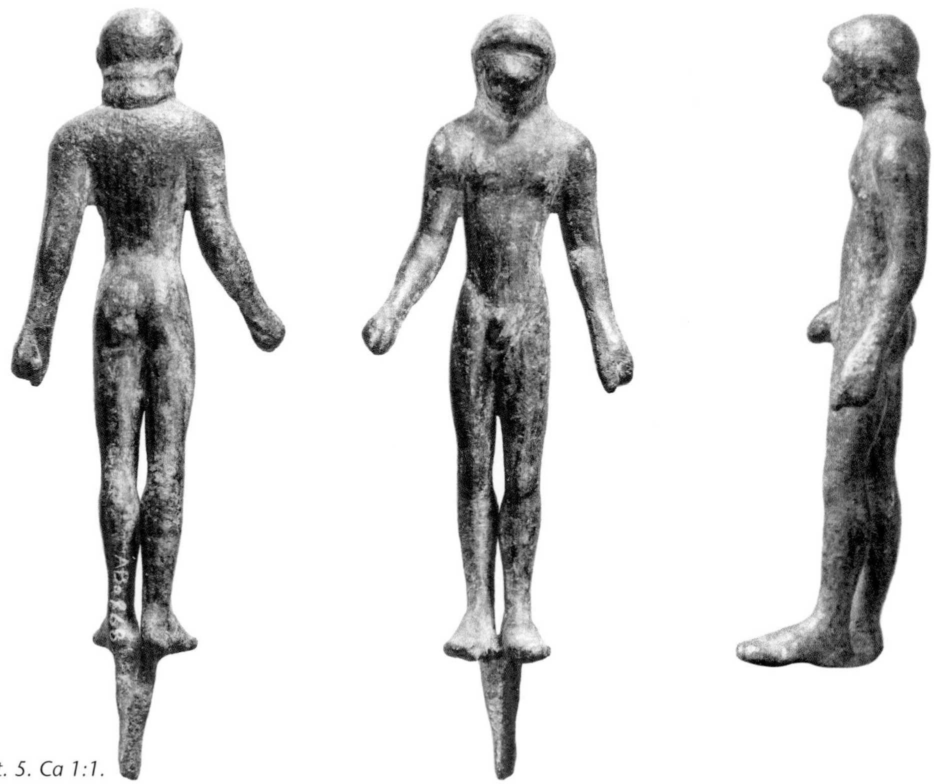

Cat. 5. Ca 1:1.

CAT. 6. STANDING MAN. TOGATUS

Inv. no. ABa 159.
H.: 11 cm.
Provenance: Unknown.
Acquisition: Bought in Florence before 1830.
Bibliography: Richardson 1983, 232 no. 2 Type 2 A; pl. 159, fig. 525. Riis 1997, 107, fig. 109; 105 note 256.
Technique: Surface very corroded and pitted. Green and brown patina. Lower part of legs and feet missing.

Beardless man standing on right leg, with left leg a little advanced. Dressed in cloak draped over left shoulder. Ends hang down in zig-zag folds over left thigh, with an open space between the two parts reaching a little below the knee. Vague traces of decorated borders. Left arm akimbo, index finger stretched forward, thumb backward, middle fingers bent toward palm, right hand with cylindrical hole for now missing object, held near waist. Shoulders very broad, narrow hips, long pronounced thighs. Buttocks prominent. Hair arranged in a flat fringe over forehead and falling down over shoulders in triangular mass with faint indication of curl ends. Ears superimposed on the hair. Skull egg-shaped. Low forehead. Large bulging almond-shaped eyes, full smiling lips, receding chin.

Cf Giglioli 1935, pl. 85,4, from Isola di Fano, Fossombrone, Arch.Mus. Florence inv. 72725, = Richardson 1983, pl.163, figs.539-540. Walters 1899 no.509, pl. XVI, from Pizzirimonte near Prato. = Richardson 1983, figs. 526-528. Richardson 1953, 118, fig. 34, (Cleveland), early Fifth Century BC. Galli 1918, 211, figs. 1-2, from Impruneta (Florence inv.87494). Cristofani 1985, 142, no. 30, Naples NM 5534, from Elba. Cristofani 1985, no. 7.2, from the sanctuary of Villa Cassarini (Bologna, Mus.Civ.). Richardson 1983, pl. 154, fig. 510, Basel 514. For style of head, Sprenger/Bartoloni 1977, figs. 146-147 (Lorenzini head), from Volterra. Cristofani 1979, 85-92.

Comment

There are no very close parallels to be found in other published togati, of which several have been found in Northern Etruria. There is a certain affinity to the head of the kouros statuette from Impruneta, which presumably is part of a votive deposit belonging to a nearby sanctuary. The hairstyle is similar to that of the naked hand-on-hip statuette Florence inv. 93 (Richardson 1983, figs. 516-517). The closest parallel for general style and proportions is the naked kouros Basel 514 (Richardson 1983, figs. 154), which also has a similar, if not identical, way of putting the fingers on the hip. This statuette is ascribed to the "Populonia Group" by Jucker (Jucker 1970, 209 f., figs. 27 a-h), and the Copenhagen togatus may be another member of this group. Richardson places the Basel bronze in her Middle Archaic Period, but has the Impruneta kouros in Late Archaic (Richardson 1983, p. 226; 228). The feature of the complicated position of the hand and the drapery of ABa 159 point to a date late in the Sixth Century BC. Riis (1997, 105), however, favours a Clusine workshop.

Northwest Etruscan. Populonia or Clusium.
End of Sixth Century BC.

Cat. 6.

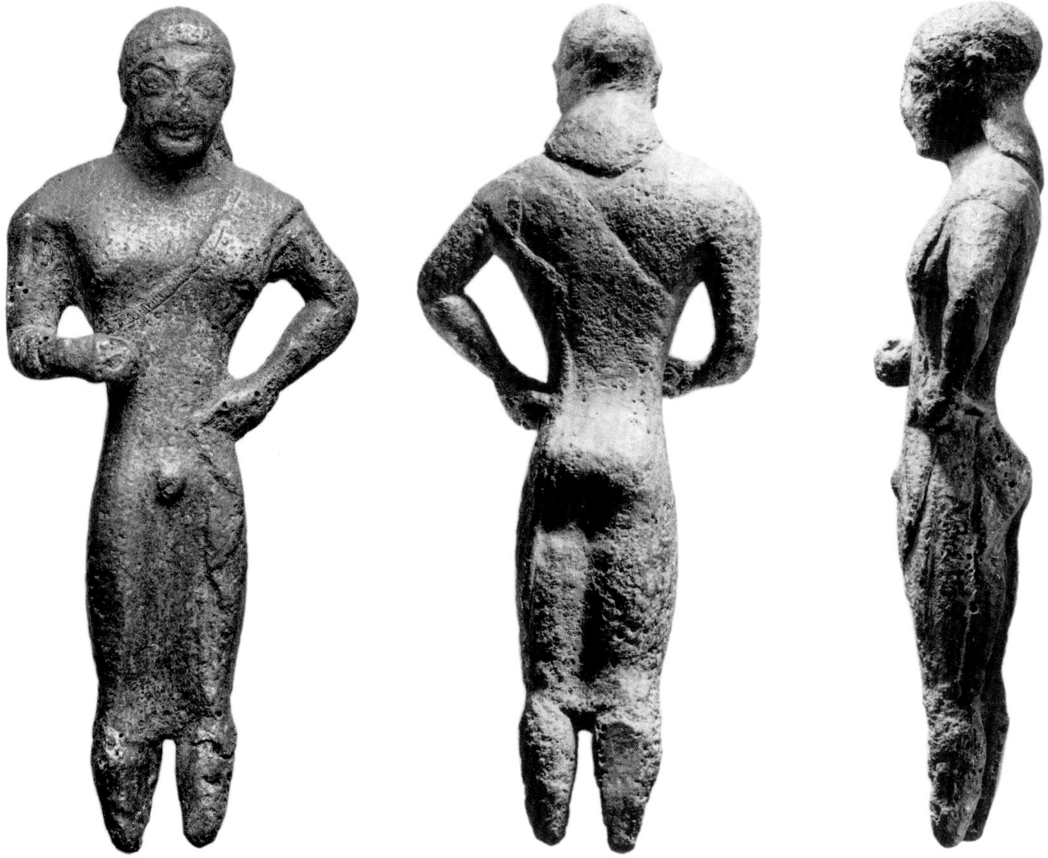

Cat. 6. Ca 1:1.

CAT. 7. WARRIOR. SPEARMAN TYPE

Inv. no. 9831.
H.: 10,4 cm.
Provenance: Found 1907 at Villa Santa Maria a Mare at Porto San Giorgio, Macerata (Marche).
Acquisition: June 1937. Bought from private collector.
Bibliography: Riis 1941, 203f. note 5. Riis 1946, 46 note 14; Riis 1957, 37, note 17. Briguet 1959, 134, no. 3, fig. 5. Balty 1961, 53 Group D no.1. Richardson 1983, 63 no. 6; 75. Series C Group 2.
Technique: Surface uneven and corroded. Dark green and brown patina.

Youth wearing triangular perizoma fastened by belt at the back above the buttocks. Standing with both feet on a flat base with a large nail through it. The left leg slightly advanced. Left arm akimbo, right stretched forward, with large cylindrical hole in hand for weapon, now missing. Broad shoulders, narrow hips, long, slender legs. The thighs are joined in the casting to above knees. Pronounced calves. Hair arranged in fringe and mass hanging down the neck, coming down into a point. Crown of head flat, low forehead, large bulging eyes, receding chin.

Cf Mazzolai 1958, 195 fig. 2. (Grosseto no. 1198). Lebel 1961, pl. XXXVII,1 no. 71 (A 385) (close). Jucker 1970, 202 f., fig.14 (Brussels R 938,1), from Chiusi. Richardson 1983, 223, no. 14, description p. 230 (Oxford Ashmolean Museum B 22). *Eadem* 1983, 63, Series C, Group 2 no. 4, pl. 36, figs. 141-143 (Volterra 1/52/B); 74 Series C, Group 1 no. 2 (Florence 65 (130).

Comment

An example of Richardson's "Spearmen Group", and fairly close to Volterra 1/52/B. It is, however, even closer to Florence 65 (130), her Series C, Spearmen Group 1 no.2. She does find the figures of both groups close in style, and perhaps there is no reason to distinguish between them. The group is placed by her in the second quarter of the Sixth Century BC.

North Etruscan.
575-550 BC.

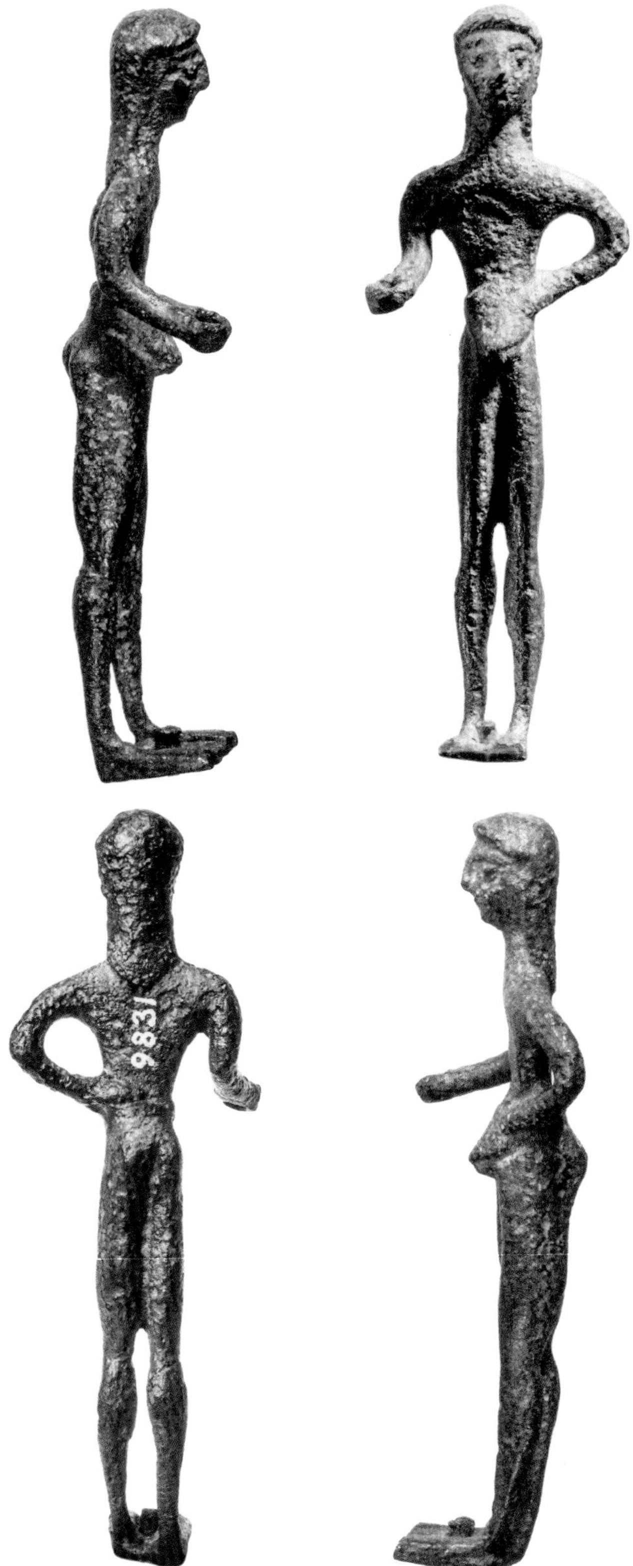

Cat. 7. Ca 1:1.

CAT. 8. WARRIOR. SWORDSMAN TYPE

Inv. no. 13173.
H.: 6,5 cm.
Provenance: Said to have been found at Carthage.
Acquisition: Bought in 1951 in the art market.
Bibliography: Briguet 1959, 132-133 no. 3, fig. 1. Balty 1961, p. 57 no. 36. Richardson 1983, 62 Series A, Group 2 no. 13; 68 no. 13.
Technique: Surface matt. Vivid green patina in places, otherwise dark green.

Cat. 8. Ca 1:1.

Warrior wearing double perizoma, standing with both feet wide apart on circular base. The shoulders are very broad. The upper torso tapering into a narrow waist. The thighs are short and round. The lower legs form a sharp line in front, likely to indicate greaves, also rendered by a thickening at the calves. Naked feet straight forward, toes indicated. Right arm held forward, bent at the elbow. Fingers vaguely marked. On the inside of the flat hand traces of the weapon he has held. Left arm broken off over elbow. Large head, flat crown. Hair divided in the middle and combed to each side, falling down the neck in thick mass, ends marked by short vertical furrows. Line indicating fillet. Low forehead, straight eyebrows, bulging eyes, pronounced cheek-bones, protruding and smiling mouth, prominent chin.

Cf de Ridder 1913, pl. 12 (Louvre no. 105, said to be from Crete). Riis 1941, 120 f., pl. 21,1, Florence no. 42. Fogolari 1950-51, pl.II, h-i centre row (Verona). Richardson 1983, 68 no. 15 (St.Germain-en-Laye); 68 no. 12, (Clermont-Ferrand, Musée Bargoin); 67 no. 8, pl. 27, figs. 107-109 (Volterra 26); also pl. 107, figs. 375-376, with helmet (Florence 91.381). Cristofani 1985, 128 no. 11, (Florence no. 47); 126 no.9 (Arezzo no. 11.495), very close; 131 no. 15 (Leiden H 3 ZZZZ 5, from Montalcino); 132 no. 17 (Karlsruhe Badisches Landesmuseum F 1767, very close). Maggiani 1991, 986 f., figs. 1-3 (Florence inv. 110582), from Volterra, Porta S. Felice.

Comment

This type of warrior has some features derived from Greek representations of devotees, *eg* the criophoros Berlin 7477 from Crete (Rolley 1967, pl. 11,41), with which it shares the large head, the parting of the hair and the wearing of a loincloth, but from which it differs considerably in general style, especially in the short stocky legs. With the Etruscan warriors in Arezzo, Leiden and Karlsruhe it also has the hairstyle in common. In proportions and facial features it comes closest to the latter and it is presumably from the same workshop.

North Etruscan.
625-600 BC.

CAT. 9. WARRIOR WITH SPEAR

Inv. no. 516.
H.: 11,3 cm.
Provenance: Unknown.
Acquisition: 1871. Bought in Milan.
Bibliography: Unpublished.
Technique: Surface matt. Green patina. Under feet tangs, now shortened. Spear broken, but preserved.

Cat. 9. Ca. 1:1.

Warrior hurling spear in raised right hand, left arm lowered and advanced, a now missing object (shield) having been riveted to the hand. Weight on advanced left leg, right leg set back, but bent due to faulty casting. Naked. Big toe on left foot indicated by furrow. Breast muscles and lower edges of abdomen indicated. Attic helmet with lowered cheek-pieces. Ears exposed. Large crest, the lower part of which is joined to the back of the statuette. Eyes almond-shaped with raised lids. Full, smiling mouth. Beardless, round chin.

Cf Cristofani 1985, 83 no. 2,7, (Florence inv. 566); 84 no. 2,8, (Florence inv. 565) both from deposito di Broglio, Val di Chiana. Richardson 1983, 177, pl. 118 fig. 406 (BM 452), (Late Archaic, Series A Group 2), for stance, general proportions and details of abdomen, from Amelia, Umbria; pl. 114 fig. 392, with tunic (Louvre 125) (Middle Archaic, Series B, Ionians, no. 3), from Central Italy.

Comment

This kind of attacking warrior is fairly rare. The examples in the Florence Museum inv. 566 and 565 from the Brolio deposit are much larger. They both represent a helmeted warrior hurling his spear in the raised right arm, while the left arm is bent, holding a now missing shield. Inv. 566, who is wearing a cuirass over a short tunic, is advancing quietly, whereas inv. 565, who is naked, is running. Cat. 9 (inv. 516) shares these two features with the latter, but the legs are closer together and the style is quite different, the Copenhagen warrior showing a pronounced roundness in face and body, more in the Ionian tradition, not unlike the warrior wearing a tunic and helmet, Louvre 125. The large warrior Florence 586 (Cristofani 1985, 191 no.87) with chiton and cuirass is obviously much later ("severe"), and even later is the naked Greek warrior from Aphiona on Corfu (Bulle 1930, pl. XII).

Umbrian (?).
Last third of Sixth Century BC.

CAT. 10. WARRIOR
Inv. no. ABa 469.
H. without tang: 6,5 cm. H. with tang: 7,9 cm.
Provenance: Unknown.
Acquisition: 1946. Bought in Italy.
Bibliography: Unpublished.
Technique: Tang under right foot. Surface matt. Green patina. Missing: weapon, left leg from knee.

Schematic naked striding warrior with left leg advanced. Right arm lowered and held back. In hand a hole for weapon. On left shoulder round shield, arm not indicated. Deep furrow separate forehead from helmet (?) or hair. Face angular. Notch indicating mouth. Punched circles for eyes and nipples.

Cf Lebel 1961 pl. XXXVII,2. Colonna 1970, pl. 68, no. 242, from Amelia, Umbria.

Cat. 10. Ca. 1:1

Comment
Colonna refrains from connecting this common type of schematic warrior with a specific type of larger sculpture, but thinks it especially adapted to the small format. Obviously these very schematic votives, that may have been produced over a long period, cannot be dated, unless their context is known, but they are hardly older than the Fifth Century BC, and many possibly much later.

South Umbrian.
Fifth Century BC or later?

Cat. 11. Striding man
Inv. no. ABa 470d.
H. with tangs: 6,2 cm. Without tangs: 5,5 cm.
Provenance: Unknown.
Acquisition: 1846. Bought in Rome.
Bibl: Unpublished.
Technique: Smooth surface. Dark brown patina. Filing marks.

Schematic striding male, arms stretched out. Feet turned to the left. Punched circles for eyes, nipples and navel. Prominent sex.

Cf Cat.10 (ABa 469).

South Umbrian.
Fifth Century BC or later.

Cat. 11. Ca. 1:1

CAT. 12. STRIDING MAN

Inv. no. ABa 564
H. without tangs: 9,3 cm. H. with tangs: 10,7 cm.
Provenance: Unknown.
Acquisition: 1853. Bought in Rome.
Bibliography: Unpublished.
Technique: Fairly smooth surface. Green patina. Tangs under feet.

Schematic, naked striding warrior with left leg and arm advanced, right arm held back. Fingers and toes indicated. Possibly wearing helmet. Punched circles for eyes, nipples and navel. Sex indicated.

Cf Lebel 1961, pl. XXXVII,2. Colonna 1970, pl. 66, no. 248, from Amelia, Umbria; pl. 67, no. 237, Group" Amelia" (close). Richardson 1983, pl. 106, fig. 371 (Brussels A 475).

Adam 1984 no. 265, prov. "Vielle Toulouse", (Fifth Century BC). Fogolari 1950-51, pl. 2, centre row.

Comment

Richardson (1983, 162) regards this very common type as being derived from Late Archaic kouroi in an attitude of prayer, but in view of the dynamic stance it may be more relevant to consider the affinity with warrior types like the preceding Cat.11 (ABa 469) in the same stance and provided with a shield.

Cat. 12. Ca. 1:1.

South Umbrian.
Fifth Century BC and later.

CAT. 13. STRIDING MAN

Without inv. no.
H.: 6,3 cm without tangs.
Provenance: Unknown.
Acquisition: Unknown.
Bibliography: Unpublished.
Technique: Surface smooth, but a little pitted. Dark green patina. Filing marks.

Flat naked male standing with legs widely apart. Very short arms stretched out to the sides. Fingers indicated at ends. Head cubic, with deep furrows separating face from scull. Punched circles for eyes, nipples and navel. Prominent sex.

Cf Cat. 12 (ABa 564); Colonna 1970, pl. 73 no. 319 (Group Esquilino).

Comment

This piece might be part of the Esquiline votive deposit, originally containing sixty figurines, of which fourteen specimens are now in Museo Pigorini.

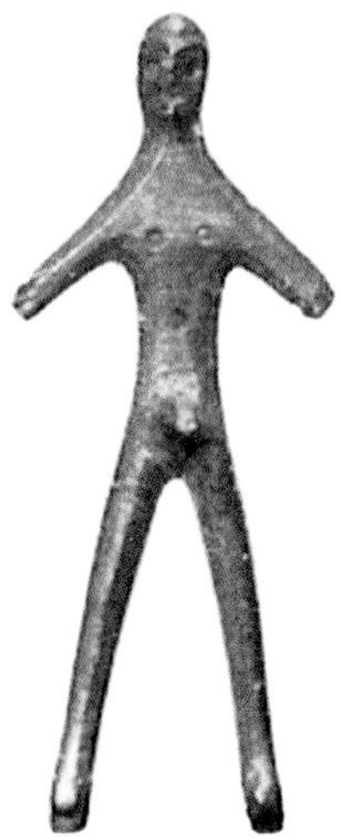

Cat. 13. Ca. 1:1.

Fifth-Fourth Century BC. (?)

CAT. 14. CUIRASSED WARRIOR

Without inv. no.
H.: 6,5 cm.
Provenance: Unknown.
Acquisition: Unknown.
Bibliography: Unpublished.
Technique: Surface smooth in parts. Olive-green patina.
Missing: Right hand with weapon, left arm from elbow, right lower leg and foot.

Striding warrior brandishing weapon in raised right arm, left arm lowered and advanced. Dressed in soft cuirass coming down to the thighs. Head tilted to the left. Large eyes, prominent nose, broad lips. Hair indicated by short radiating strokes.

Cf for prototype Cat. 16 (inv. 6578) and Cat. 17 (inv. ABa 155). Colonna 1970, pl. 29 no. 114, (North Umbria). *Culture adriatiche* 1978, pl. 180, from Chieti.

North Umbrian (?)
Third Century BC or later.

Cat. 14. Ca. 1:1.

CAT. 15. NAKED WARRIOR

Inv. no. 1250a.
H: 9,9 cm. H. of tang: 0,9 cm. H. With longer tang: 10,8 cm.
Provenance: Unknown.
Acquisition: Given by Mrs. Bech in 1878/79.
Bibliography: Unpublished.
Technique: Smooth surface. Dark green to black patina. Left arm missing from shoulder. Tangs under both feet, one partly broken off.

Naked warrior wearing helmet with low crest coming down the neck at the back. Standing on right leg, left leg advanced, leaning forward. Brandishing now missing weapon in raised right hand, which has a large hole. Long flattish torso without modelling. Prominent sex. Hardly any facial features.

Cf Colonna 1970, p. 66 no. 224 (prov. Amelia).

South Umbrian.
Fifth Century BC or later.

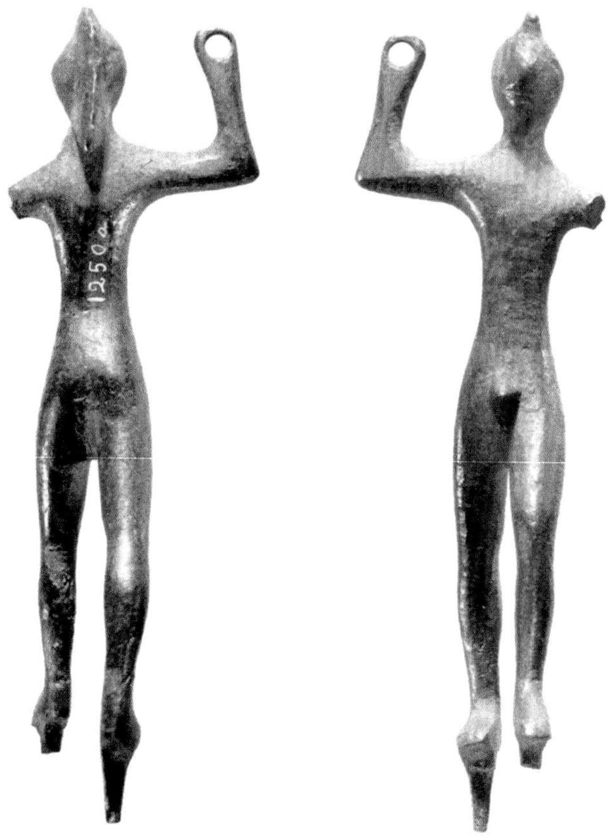

Cat. 15. Ca. 1:1.

CAT. 16. WARRIOR (MARTE ITALICO)
Inv. no. 6578.
H. without tangs: 21 cm. Tangs: Ca. 5 cm
Provenance: Terni.
Acquisition: 1910. Bought in Rome.
Bibliography: Unpublished.
Technique: Surface smooth. Under feet large tangs.
Olive-green to brown patina.

Striding beardless warrior, hurling weapon in right raised hand with cylindrical hole for now missing weapon. Left arm held out, hand clenched, fingers marked. Dressed in close-fitting cuirass with dotted lines and punched circles limiting shoulder flaps without decoration. Around waist plastic girdle. One row of pteryges with incised crosses, underneath another row with punched circles. No tunic. Knemides with row of circles along edges, also on the back, showing joining of edges. Helmet with raised cheekpieces. On both sides of large crest alternating dotted wavy lines and punched circles converging toward the head. At the bottom of the crest a row of wolf's teeth. The triangular front part of the helmet has a row of punched circles along upper edge and three horizontally placed circles over bottom edge. Large, sharply cut nose, very large eyes with bulging eye-balls and raised lids. Right eye placed higher than the left. Dimple in upper lip. Full lips. Small pointed chin. Prominent sex.

Cf de Ridder 1913, 25.279 (prov."Haute-Italie"). Bendinelli 1920, 221 ff., pl.2. Rodin Collectioneur, no. 199, pl. 77 Fourth Century BC). Strong 1968, 105, left, (Mansell Coll. very close, from the Perugia region). Colonna 1970, 76 no. 175, pl. 50 (BM 444). (Southern Umbria, group "Todi") (close); pl. 36 no. 138 (Oxford Fortnum B 7). Richardson 1983, pl. 124 figs. 421-422 (Oxford Fortnum B 6); pl. 122, figs. 418-419 (Villa Giulia 6721). Adam 1984 nos. 255; 257.

Comment
This warrior is another member of Colonna's Todi group, being quite close to BM 444 from the Towneley Collection, ascribed by Colonna to his Maestro A. There are a few differences in the details of the cuirass and the Danish National Museum specimen wears no tunic.

None of the warriors having been found in context the dating is exclusively based on stylistic criteria. Richardson refers for the helmets and cuirasses to Attic vase painting of the early Fifth Century BC. Colonna feels confident that a date in the second half of the Fifth Century is correct.

Cat. 16. Ca. 80%

South Umbrian.
450-400 BC or later.

Cat. 16. Ca. 80%

CAT. 17. WARRIOR (MARTE ITALICO)
Inv. no. ABa 155.
H. without tangs: 19 cm. Tangs: 3-3,2 cm.
Provenance: Found by fishermen on the bank of Lago di Bevagna, locally called l'Abisso (Umbria), in March 1774. It was sent to Perugia, where a learned "Sig. Genghini, luogotenente di quel governo" wrote a dissertation on the statuette, which was then incorporated in Museo Cenci. This dissertation was copied by Bartolomeo Cenci and is now in the archives of the Danish National Museum. According to this document the Cenci Museum sold the statuette to Domenico Bargili from Ravenna. A further postscript by Chr.T. Falbe states that he has bought it from the antique dealer Avvocato Rusca in Florence in February 1828.
Acquisition: Bought in 1828 from Coll. Rusca, Florence.
Bibliography: Colonna 1970, 116, no. VI.
Technique: Under feet large tangs. Brown patina. Surface quite well-preserved, a few slightly corroded areas.

Cat. 17. Ca. 80%

Striding beardless warrior, left leg advanced, hurling spear in raised right hand. The left hand is held out from the body, ending in a flat triangle indubitably meant to hold a shield. The torso is tilted to the left and forms a strongly curved arch with the hip line.

He wears a tightfitting cuirass with short sleeves, incised with vertical rows of double arches on front and back. Dotted lines for neck-line, vertical joining of cuirass and triangular shoulder flaps, the latter decorated with four punched circles. Around waist plastic notched girdle. This is more likely than it being the end of the cuirass, which seems to continue into three tiers of *pteryges* of diminishing size, the top one decorated with two rows of double arches, the middle one with groups of vertical lines and the bottom one with one row of double arches. No tunic. The helmet has raised cheek pieces and a huge crest incised with double arches at base on one side and circles on the other. The main area of the crest decorated with herringbone pattern in dotted lines on both sides. On legs *knemides* also covering knees. Toes indicated.

The face has a very prominent, sharply cut nose, large full lips, small sharply cut chin. Large eyesockets, in which almond-shaped eyes with strongly marked eyelids.

Cf de Ridder 1913, I, pl. 25 n o. 279 (close). Walters 1899 no. 444. Colonna 1970, no. 180, pl. 52 (Villa Giulia without no., from Calvi dell'Umbria (Maestro B); no. 181, pls. 54-56 (Pesaro, Museo Oliveriano inv. 3323, from Todi) (Maestro B); no. 187, pls. 57-59 (Perugia Arch.Mus. inv. 603, Coll. Guardabassi, said to be from Ancarano, (near Maestro B).

Comment
Quite close to Colonna's Group Todi, Maestro B, although there are differences in the facial features, the tilting of the upper torso toward the left and the incised decoration.

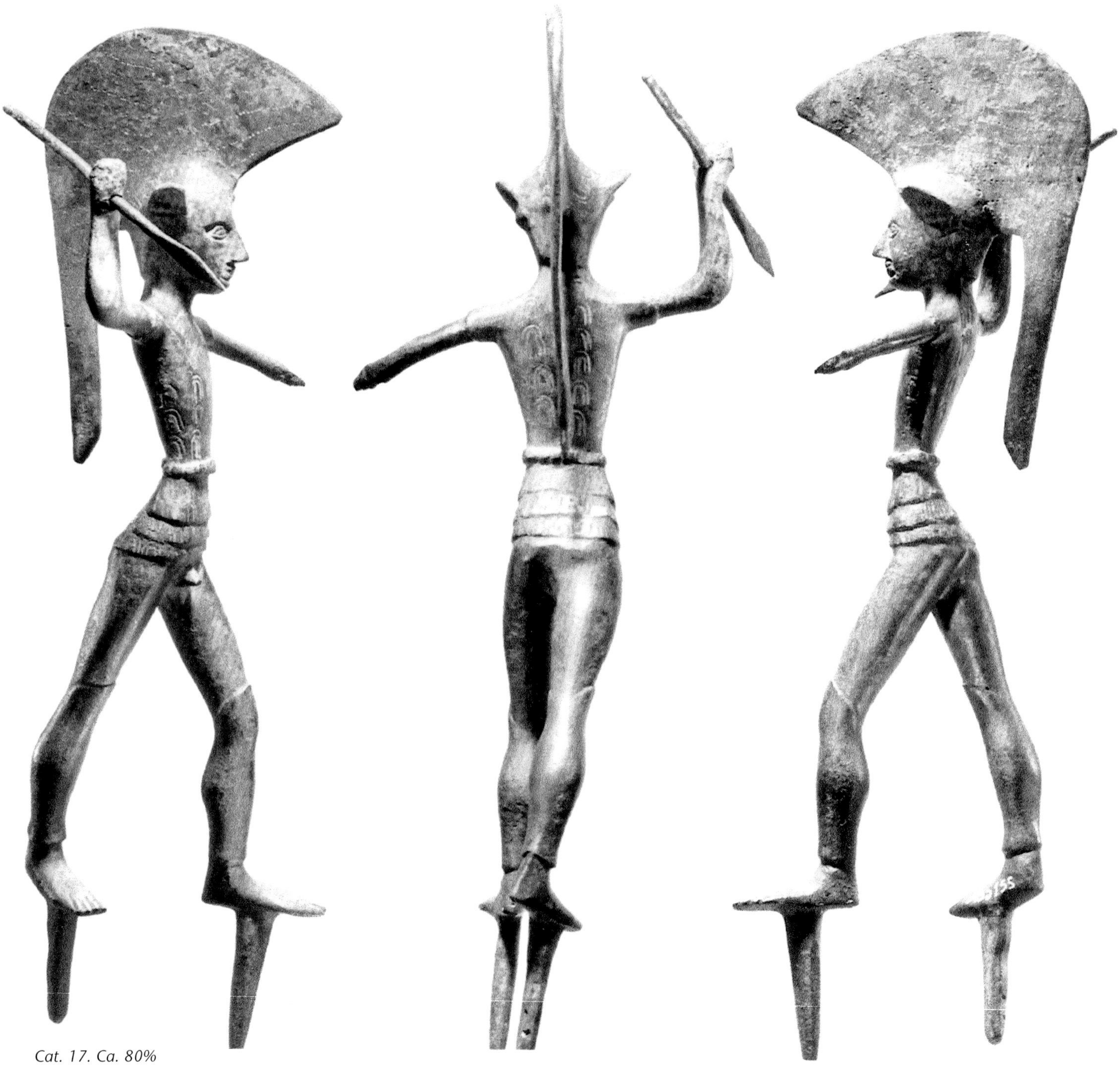

Cat. 17. Ca. 80%

There are also affinities to Colonna's Maestro A, *eg* to the warrior BM 444. The incised decoration of the cuirass is close to Louvre 279.

South Umbria.
450-400 BC or later.

CAT. 18. CUIRASSED WARRIOR

Inv. no. ABa 158.
Provevance: Unknown.
H.: 10,1 cm.
Acquisition: 1828. Bought by Falbe in Florence.
Bibliography: Unpublished.
Technique: Missing left arm from under shoulder. Dark brown and green patina.

Cat. 18. Ca. 1:1

Warrior hurling now missing weapon in raised right hand, which has a cylindrical hole. Weight of figure on right leg, left leg slightly bent and advanced. The figure is leaning backwards. Left buttock higher than the right. Wearing cuirass with dots and spiral incisions indicating shoulder flaps, and ending in *pteryges*. Dots along neckline. Possible indication of sleeve on right arm. Lower body naked. *Knemides* covering knees indicated by faint lines. Toes indicated. Helmet with dotted lines alternating with punched circles along right edge of helmet, under which the hair shows at the back. Large square face, large eyes, small nose, full lips, slightly smiling.

Cf de Ridder 1913, pl. 25 no. 277 (close) Richardson 1983, pl. 125 fig. 424 (Vienna 52); 185, pl. 128 fig. 433 (Brussels R 859-1, from votive deposit found near Foligno about 1859). *AnnMuseoFaina* XI, 2004, 143, fig. 25, votive deposit found at Gravisca.

Richardson compares the facial features of the Foligno warriors with those of the "Pretty Mannerists", *eg* the kore Danish National Museum 946 (Cat. 55), but the warrior ABa 158 is less smiling, and his body, with the marked difference of the level of the buttocks, points to a somewhat later date.

Comment

The warrior ABa 158 does not fit into any of Colonna's groups of Italic warriors, most of which are characterized by a cuirass finishing in a rounded belt, often have three rows of *pteryges* and are wearing a helmet with raised cheek-pieces, *eg* Colonna 1970, no. 138, pl. XXXVI. In contrast, Aba 158 has a cuirass that ends directly in one row of *pteryges*. It is not quite clear whether the artist is referring to a metal cuirass or one made of a softer material.The closest parallel so far is the statuette from Gravisca, found together with a bronze kouros, miniature weapons made of iron or bronze and several female protomes of Magna-Graecian or Sicilian style. This warrior has a cuirass with longer *pteryges*, which looks like the archaic Greek cuirass worn by one of the hoplites of the Vix krater, Rolley 1984, 138 figs. 128-129 and by two of the warriors of the East frieze of the Siphnian Treasury, Stuart 1990, figs. 193-194. There is also an affinity to the archaic hoplite statuette from the sanctuary of Athena from Francavilla near Sybaris, Rolley 1984, fig. 259.

South Umbrian
480-450 BC.

SCHEMATIC MALE FIGURES

CAT. 19. SCHEMATIC WARRIOR

Inv. no. 8359.
H.: 12,6 cm.
Provenance: Unknown.
Acquisition: In 1924. Given by the Ny Carlsberg Foundation.
Bibliography: Unpublished.
Technique: Surface smooth. Dark green patina. Under feet partly remaining tangs. Left arm broken off over elbow.

Schematic striding warrior with large crest. Face angular with punched circle for eye. Mouth and chin indicated. Punched circles for nipples and navel. Sex prominent. Lowered right hand has circular hole for missing weapon.

Cf Bendinelli 1920, c. 234 fig. 10 (deposito di Cagli). Stefani 1935, 158 fig. 3a (votive deposit found at Gualdo Tadino in 1935). Colonna 1970, no. 269 (Brussels R 859 from votive deposit found near Foligno in 1858) (Group "Foligno" Series B; see also no.163 with bibliography, for circumstances of finding. Monacchi 1988, pl. 35,c, votive deposit of Grotta Bella (Terni), "Group Nocera Umbra", (very close). *Gens antiquissima Italiae* 1991, 218 f., no. 4.28, from the 1990 excavations at Monte Acuto, Umbertide.

Cat. 19. Ca. 1:1

Comment

The sanctuary at Gualdo Tadino continued until Roman times. The votive deposit at Umbertide covers a period from the end of the Sixth to the beginning of the Fourth Century BC. The main activity in Grotta Bella occurred from the Third to the Second Century BC, but was possibly also in use earlier.

South Umbrian.
Third to Second Century BC.

CAT. 20. SCHEMATIC WARRIOR
Inv. no. 8360.
H. without tangs: 12,4 cm. With tangs: 14 cm.
Provenance: Unknown.
Acquisition: In1924. Given by the Ny Carlsberg Foundation.
Bibliography: Unpublished.
Technique: Surface matt. Dark green patina. Under feet tangs. Solder repair at waist.

Flat schematic warrior, striding with both arms stretched out, right arm ending in hook for insertion of now missing weapon. Helmet with large semicircular crest, separated from head by horizontal groove. Eyes and nipples indicated by punched circles.

Cf Cat. 19 - Cat. 28. Oxford 3280.1887. Giglioli 1935, pl. 222,6 (Villa Giulia). Colonna 1970, pl. 70, nos. 264; 269 (Brussels R 859 from votive deposit found in 1858 near Foligno).

Comment
A specimen belonging to Colonna's Group "Foligno" Series B.

South Umbrian.
Third-Second Century BC.

Cat. 20. Ca. 1:1

CAT. 21. SCHEMATIC WARRIOR
Inv. no. ABa 468a.
H. without tang: 8,2 cm. With tang: 9,4 cm.
Provenance: Unknown.
Acquisition: 1846. Bought in Italy.
Bibliography: Unpublished.
Technique: Surface smooth. Black patina. Tangs under feet.

Flat schematic striding warrior with large crest. Hole in right arm for weapon. Head cubic with sharp nose ridge. Mouth indicated by notch. Punched circles for eyes, nipples and navel. Sex prominent.

Comment
The specimen from Amelia, Colonna's Group "Foligno", Series C especially close.

Southern Umbrian.
Third-Second Century BC.

Cat. 21. Ca. 1:1

CAT. 22. SCHEMATIC WARRIOR
Inv. no. ABa 468c.
H.: 11 cm.
Provenance: Unknown.
Acquisition: 1846. Bought in Italy.
Bibliography: Unpublished.
Technique: Surface matt and corroded. Dark green and brown patina. Missing: left arm and leg, end of right leg.

Flat schematic striding warrior with large crest. Hole in right hand for weapon. Sides of face meeting in a sharp angle over nose. Punched circles indicate eyes. Pattern of lines and dots on crest, mostly covered by corrosion.

Cf Cat 19-28. Colonna 1970, pl. 70 nos. 268-269 (Group "Foligno", Series B); 273, (do., Series C).

South Umbrian.
Third-Second Century BC.

Cat. 22. Ca. 1:1

CAT. 23. SCHEMATIC WARRIOR

Inv. no. ABa 468b.
H.: 7,7 cm.
Provenance: Unknown.
Acquisition: 1846. Bought in Italy.
Bibliography: Unpublished.
Technique: Surface fairly smooth. Dark greyish patina. Most of left leg missing. Cut out of bronze sheet. Filing marks.

Flat schematic warrior with semicircular crest. Both arms stretched out and lowered. In right hand circular hole with spear made from bronze thread with flattened ends. Cubic head. Circular punches for eyes, nipples and navel. Sex indicated.

Cf Cat. 19-29. Colonna 1970, pl. 70 no. 264 from votive deposit, Foligno 1858 (Group "Foligno", Series B). *Gens Antiquissima Italiae* 1991, 218 f. no. 428, from excavation at Monte Acuto, Umbertide, 1990.

South Umbrian.
Third-Second Century BC.

Cat. 23. Ca. 1:1

CAT. 24. SCHEMATIC WARRIOR

Inv. no. 8357.
H.: 7,6 cm
Provenance: Unknown.
Acquisition: 1924 given by the Ny Carlsberg Foundation.
Bibliography: Unpublished.
Technique: Even surface. Green patina. Missing: right arm from under shoulder.

Schematic naked warrior with large crest. Striding and with arms stretched to the sides. Nipples and navel indicated by punched circles. Face flat.

Cf Cat. 19-28. Colonna 1970, pl. 70, nos. 264; 269, votive deposit found at Foligno, prov. of Perugia, in 1858.

South Umbrian.
Third-Second Century BC.

Cat. 24. Ca. 1:1

CAT. 25. SCHEMATIC WARRIOR

Inv. no. 8358.
H.: 9,3 cm.
Provenance: Unknown.
Acquisition: 1924. Given by the Ny Carlsberg Foundation.
Bibliography: Unpublished.
Technique: Even surface. Green patina.

Schematic naked warrior with large crest. Striding with arms stretched to the sides. Nipples and navel indicated by punched circles. Face flat.

Cf Cat. 24 (inv.8357).

South Umbrian.
Third-Second Century BC.

Cat. 25. Ca. 1:1

CAT. 26. SCHEMATIC WARRIOR

Inv. no. 4787.
H.: 2,8 cm.
Provenance: Unknown.
Acquisition: 1897. Given by private collector. Originally bought in Rome.
Bibliography: Unpublished.
Technique: Cast. Surface smooth. Olive-green patina.

Cat. 26. Ca. 1:1

Schematic flat warrior with pointed helmet. In right arm hole for insertion of weapon.

Cf Cat.19-28. Colonna 1970, pl.73, no. 288, Group "Nocera Umbra".

South Umbrian.
Fourth-Third Century BC.

CAT. 27. SCHEMATIC WARRIOR
Inv. no. 4789.
H.: 6,8 cm.
Provenance: Unknown.
Acquisition: 1897. Given by private collector. Originally bought in Rome.
Bibliography; Unpublished.
Technique: Cast. Filing marks. Surface matt, in parts corroded and pitted. Green and brown patina. Ends of arms and most of right leg broken off.

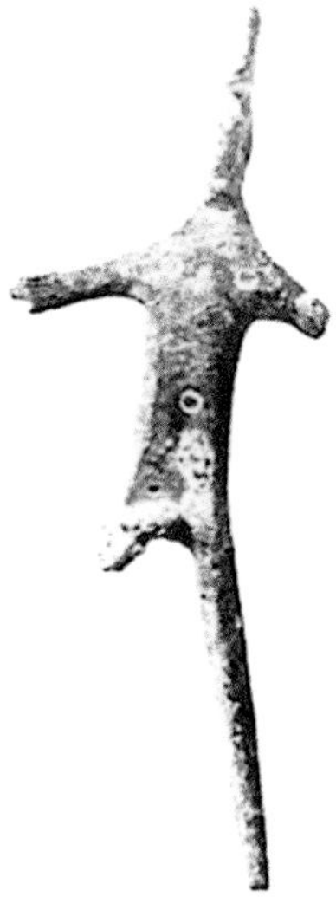
Cat. 27. Ca. 1:1

Flat, schematic warrior with crest. Punched circles for eyes, nipples and navel. Sex indicated.

Cf Cat. 19-28. Colonna 1970, pl. 73, no. 287, Group "Nocera Umbra". Monacchi 1988, pl. 35a (Group"Esquilino"), votive deposit of Grotta Bella (Terni). *Gens Antiquissima Italiae* 1991, 218 f. no. 4.28 from excavation at Monte Acuto, Umbertide, 1990.

South Umbrian.
Fourth-Third Century BC

CAT. 28. SCHEMATIC WARRIOR
Inv. no. 4788.
H.: 5,3 cm.
Provenance: Unknown.
Acquisition: 1897. Given by private collector. Originally bought in Rome.
Bibliography: Unpublished.
Technique: Cast. Surface matt, partly corroded. Vivid green patina. Missing: Ends of left arm and leg

Cat. 28. Ca. 1:1

Schematic flat warrior. Tall, narrow crest. Eyes, nipples and navel indicated by punched circles. Part of spear still in right hand. Sex prominent.

Cf Cat. 19-28. Colonna 1970, pl.73, no.288, Group "Nocera Umbra". Monacchi 1988, pl. 35a, votive deposit of Grotta Bella (Terni). *Gens Antiquissima Italiae* 1991, 218 f. no.4.28, from excavation at Monte Acuto, Umbertide, 1990.

South Umbria.
Fourth-Third Century BC.

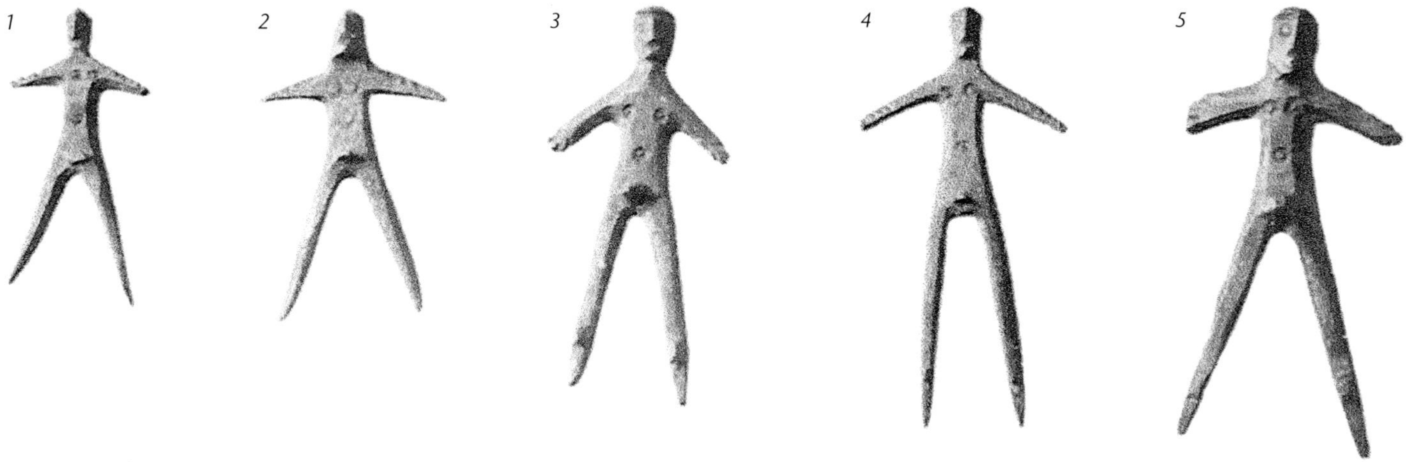

Cat. 29. Ca. 1:1.

CAT. 29. SCHEMATIC MALE FIGURINES

Inv. no. 1248 (33 pieces):
Inv. no. 1248,1. H.: 4,0 cm.
Inv. no. 1248,2. H.: 4,2 cm.
Inv. no. 1248,3. H.: 5,2 cm.
Inv. no. 1248,4. H.: 5,5 cm.
Inv. no. 1248,5. H.: 6,0 cm.
Inv. no. 1248,6. H.: 7,6 cm.
Inv .no. 1248,7. H.: 6,6 cm.
Inv. no. 1248,8. H.: 5,0 cm.
Inv. no. 1248,9. H.: 5,4 cm.
Inv. no. 1248,10. H.: 5,1 cm.
Inv. no. 1248,11. H.: 4,3 cm.
Inv. no. 1248,12. H.: 3,9 cm.
Inv. no. 1248,13. H.: 4,0 cm.
Inv. no. 1248,14. H.: 4,1 cm.
Inv. no. 1248,15. H.: 4,6 cm.
Inv. no. 1248,16. H.: 4,0 cm.
Inv. no. 1248,17. H.: 4,3 cm.
Inv. no. 1248,18. H.: 5,7 cm.
Inv. no. 1248,19. H.: 4,1 cm.
Inv. no. 1248,20. H.: 4,4,cm.
Inv. no. 1248,21. H.: 4,1 cm.
Inv. no. 1248,22. H.: 4,1 cm.
Inv. no. 1248,23. H.: 3,9 cm.
Inv. no. 1248,24. H.: 3,5 cm.
Inv. no. 1248,25 (Broken into two pieces). H.: 5,8 cm.
Inv. no. 1248,26. H.: 5,3 cm.
Inv. no. 1248,27. H.: 3,9 cm.
Inv. no. 1248,28. H.: 3,6 cm.
Inv. no. 1248,29. H.: 3,9 cm.
Inv. no. 1248,30. H.: 3,6 cm.
Inv. no. 1248,31. H.3,6 cm.
Inv. no. 1248,32. H.: 3,6 cm.
Inv. no. 1248,33. H.: 2,5 cm.
Provenance: Unknown.
Acquisition: 1878. Given by Mrs. Bech, Valbygaard. Originally bought in Rome.
Bibliography: Unpublished.
Technique: Cut-out from bronze sheet. On most pieces clear filing marks. Dark brown patina.

Schematic striding naked male figurines. Heads cubic with punched circles for eyes, nipples and navels. Sex indicated.

Cf Pinza 1905, c. 265 f., pl. 16,2-4; 8-9; 13; 15 (Coll. Nardoni). Colonna 1970, pl. 74 no. 307, sixty pieces found in a votive deposit at the Esquiline in 1876, only fourteen of which are known, now in the Museo Pigorini. Gualandi 1970, 221, fig. 3 (Marzabotto). Monacchi 1988, pl. 35a, votive deposit of Grotta Bella (Terni).

Comment

These pieces in the Danish National Museum could well be from the Esquiline deposit.

South Umbrian.
Fourth-Third Century BC.

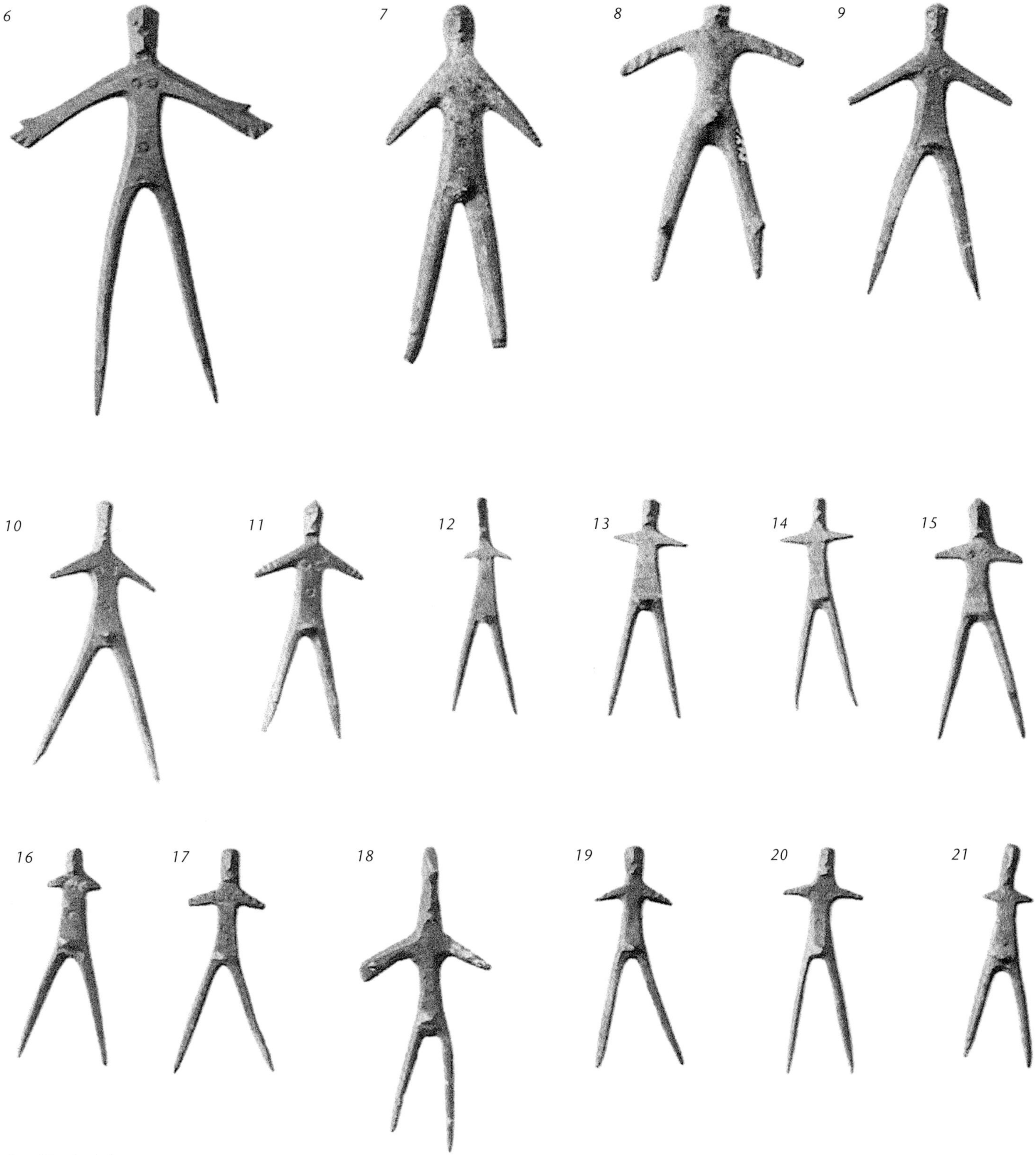

Cat. 29. Ca. 1:1.

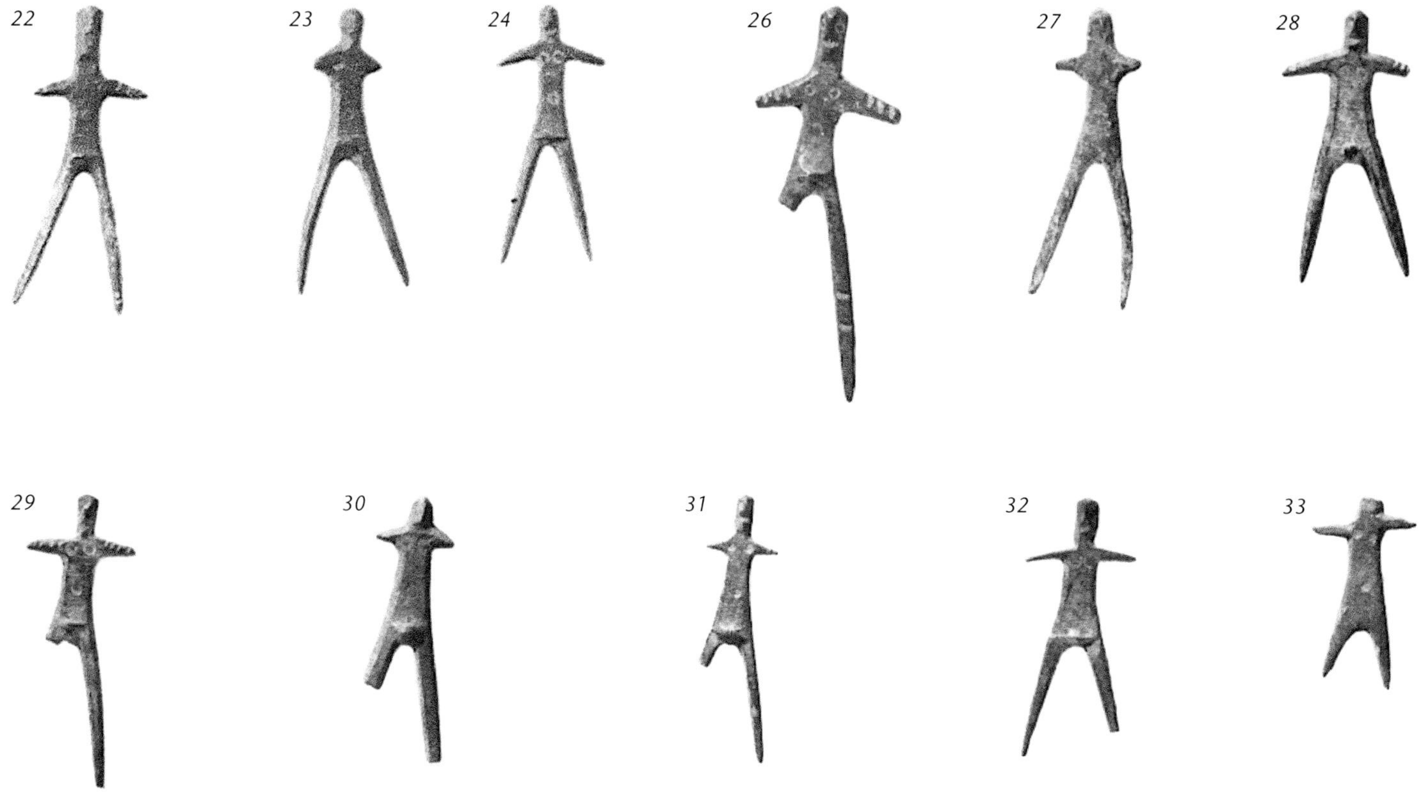

Cat. 29. Ca. 1:1.

SCHEMATIC FEMALE FIGURES

CAT. 30. STANDING FEMALE FIGURE

Without inv. no.
H. without tang: 8,0 cm.
Provenance: Unknown.
Acquisition: Unknown.
Bibliography: Unpublished.
Technique: Cast. Matt.surface. Nearly black patina. Part of left foot and tang broken off.

Schematic striding figure dressed in a long chiton. Both arms stretched to the sides, hands open, thumbs apart. Mass of hair possibly falling down to shoulders. Punched dot for navel. No facial features indicated. Head slightly tilted backwards.

Cf Budapest Inv. no. 51.155. Colonna 1970, 67 no.140; no.247, pl. 65, from Ancarano; no. 321, pl. 75, from Carsoli (Group"Esquilino"). Richardson 1983, pl. 228, figs.764; 765. Adam 1984 no. 250.

Cat. 30. Ca. 1:1.

South Umbrian.
Fourth-Third Century BC.

CAT. 31. SCHEMATIC FEMALE FIGURE

Inv. no. 4790.
H.: 6,2 cm.
Provenance: Unknown.
Acquisition: 1897. Given by private collector. Originally bought in Rome.
Bibliography: Unpublished.
Technique: Cast. Matt surface. Light green patina. Left leg broken off.

Flat schematic figure in long dress. Rudimentary arms stretched out horizontally. Long head. Deep furrow indicating hairline. Punched circles for eyes and breasts.

Cf Gens Antiquissima Italiae 1991, 212 f.; 214 f. no. 4.16, from excavation at Monte Acuto, Umbertide in 1998.

Cat. 31. Ca. 1:1.

Comment

Close to spearmen found in votive deposit belonging to the sanctuary at Monte Acuto.

South Umbrian.
Fifth-Fourth Century BC.

CAT. 32. SCHEMATIC FEMALE FIGURE

Inv. no. 4791.
H.: 4,5 cm.
Provenance: Unknown.
Acquisition: 1897. Given by private collector. Originally bought in Rome.
Bibliography: Unpublished.
Technique: Cast. Filing marks. Smooth surface. Light green patina.

Cat. 32. Ca. 1:1.

Flat figure in long dress. Arms stretched out horizontally. Long head. Punched circles for eyes, breasts and navel.

Cf Colonna 1970, no. 308, pl. 70, from votive deposit at Foligno (Group"Esquilino"). *Gens Antiquissima Italiae* 1991, 215 no. 4.18, from votive deposit at Monte Acuto, Umbertide.

South Umbrian.
Fourth Century BC.

CAT. 33. SCHEMATIC FEMALE FIGURE

Inv. no. 4794.
H.: 3,7 cm.
Provenance: Unknown.
Acquisition: 1897. Given by private collector. Originally bought in Rome.
Bibliography: Unpublished.
Technique: Cast. Filing marks. Matt, greyish-green patina.

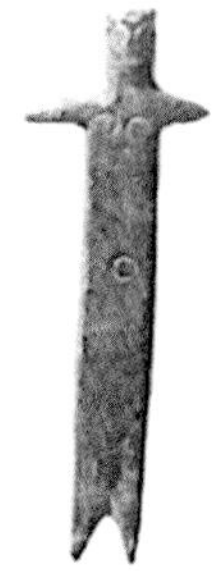

Cat. 33. Ca. 1:1.

Schematic flat figure in long dress.

Cf Cat. 32.

South Umbrian.
Fourth Century BC.

CAT. 34. SCHEMATIC FEMALE FIGURE
Inv. no. 4792.
H.: 3,3 cm.
Provenance: Unknown.
Acquisition: 1897. Given by private collector. Originally bought in Rome.
Bibliography: Unpublished.
Technique: Cast. Matt surface. Light green patina.

Cat. 34. Ca. 1:1.

Flat figure in long dress. Arms stretched out horizontally. Nipples and navel punched.

Cf Colonna 1970 no. 307, pl. 74, from the Esquiline votive deposit. *Gens Antiquissima Italiae* 1991, 215 nos. 4.16-4.18, from votive deposit found at Monte Acuto, Umbertide.

Comment
This piece might be part of the Esquiline deposit.

South Umbrian.
Fourth Century BC.

CAT. 35. SCHEMATIC FEMALE FIGURE
Inv. no. 4793.
H.: 3,5 cm.
Provenance: Unknown.
Acquisition: 1897. Given by private collector. Originally bought in Rome.
Bibliography: Unpublished.
Technique: Cast. Filing marks. Matt surface. Dark green patina.

Cat. 35. Ca. 1:1.

Flat figure in long dress. Rudimentary arms stretched out horizontally. Cubic head. Punched circles for eyes, breasts and navel.

Cf Cat. 33-34.

South Umbrian.
Fourth Century BC.

CAT. 36. SCHEMATIC FEMALE FIGURE

Inv. no. ABa 470b.
H.: 6 cm.
Provenance: Unknown.
Acquisition: 1846. Bought in Rome.
Bibliography: Unpublished.
Technique: Cast. Filing marks. Matt surface. Dark green patina. End of right leg broken off.

Schematic figure in long dress. Arms stretched out. Four indentations at ends to indicate fingers. Punched circles for eyes, nipples and navel.

Cf Cat.37. Stefani 1935, 155-173 (Gualdo Tadino).

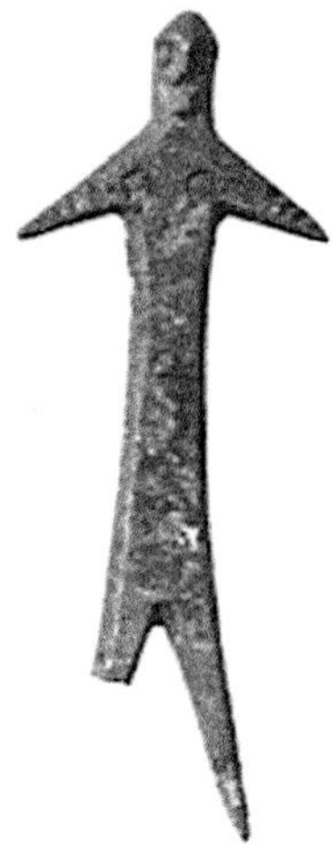

Cat. 36. Ca. 1:1.

Comment

At Gualdo Tadino foundations of a small sanctuary were excavated. In front there was a fossa about 3 m deep with schematic figurines, a great number of which also appeared inside the cella, where, allegedly, a gilt bronze foot of a statue was found. The sanctuary, which yielded eight pieces of *aes rude*, was possibly frequented from Archaic to Roman times.

South Umbrian.
Fourth Century BC.

CAT. 37. SCHEMATIC FEMALE FIGURE

Inv. no. ABa 470c.
H.: 3,7 cm.
Provenance: Unknown.
Acquisition: 1846. Bought in Rome.
Bibliography: Unpublished.
Technique: Cast. Filing marks. A few verdigris spots.

Flat figure in long dress. Short arms stretched out horizontally. Punched circles for eyes, nipples and navel.

Cf Cat. 33-35. Andrén 1967, pl. XXXIIa, Santuario della Cannicella, Orvieto. Stefani 1935, 158, fig. 3 (Gualdo Tadino). Colonna 1970 no. 307, pl. 74, votive deposit from the Esquiline 1876; no. 308, pl. 70, votive deposit near Foligno (Group"Esquilino").

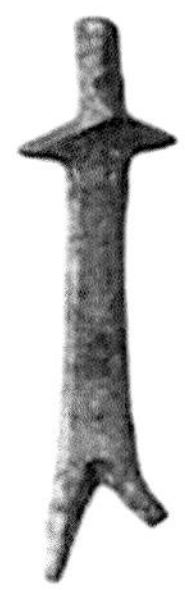

Cat. 37. Ca. 1:1.

South Umbrian.
Fourth Century BC.

CAT. 38. SCHEMATIC FEMALE FIGURE
Inv. no. ABa 470a.
H.: 5,5 cm.
Provenance: Unknown.
Acquisition: 1846. Bought in Rome.
Bibliography: Unpublished.
Technique: Cast. Filing marks. Smooth surface. Dark brown and green patina.

Schematic flat figure in long dress, under which short legs appear. Short arms stretched out obliquely, four indentations at ends, indicating fingers. Large cubic head. Deep groove indicating hairline. Punched circles for eyes, nipples and navel.

Cf Cat. 39. Colonna 1970 no. 307, pl. 74 (Group "Esquilino"). Gubbio Excavations 1984-85, Monte Asciano, *StEtr* 54, 1986 (1988), 379 f., 381, fig. 13,3.

South Umbrian.
Fourth-Third Century BC.

Cat. 38. Ca. 1:1.

CAT. 39. SCHEMATIC FEMALE FIGURES

Inv. no. 1249a-n.
H. of a: 5,2 cm; b: 5,4 cm; c: 6 cm; d: 5,7 cm; e: 5,4 cm; f: 5,6 cm; g: 6,4 cm; h: 4,9 cm; i: 4,3 cm; j: 4,1 cm; k: 4,2 cm; l: 3,6 cm; m: 5,7 cm; n: 5,9 cm.
Provenance: Unknown.
Acquisition: 1878. Given by Mrs. Bech. Originally bought in Rome.
Bibliography: Unpublished.
Technique: Cast. Filing marks. Dark brown and green patina. Surface of most specimens smooth.

Schematic flat figures in long dresses. Punched circles for eyes, nipples and navels. Some have indentations on ends of arms indicating fingers.

Cf Cederna 1951, 200 fig. 11 no. 26, from votive deposit at Carsoli. Colonna 1970 no. 313, pl. 74 (Group"Esquilino"). Scarpignato 1986, pl. IV,3-5, from Bettona (Umbria). Excavations at Gubbio 1984-85, Monte Ansciano, *StEtr* 54, 1986 (1988), 379 f., fig.13,3. Monacchi 1988, pl. 35b, votive deposit of Grotta Bella (Terni). *Gens Antiquissima Italiae* 1991, 215 f., nos. 4.16-4.19, from votive deposit at Monte Acuto di Umbertide.

Comment

As the votive deposit of Monte Acuto, Umbertide, covers a period from the end of the Sixth to the beginning of the Fourth Century BC and the Carsoli deposit starts in the last decades of the Fourth Century B C a date in the Fourth Century BC may be suggested.

South Umbrian.
Fourth Century BC.

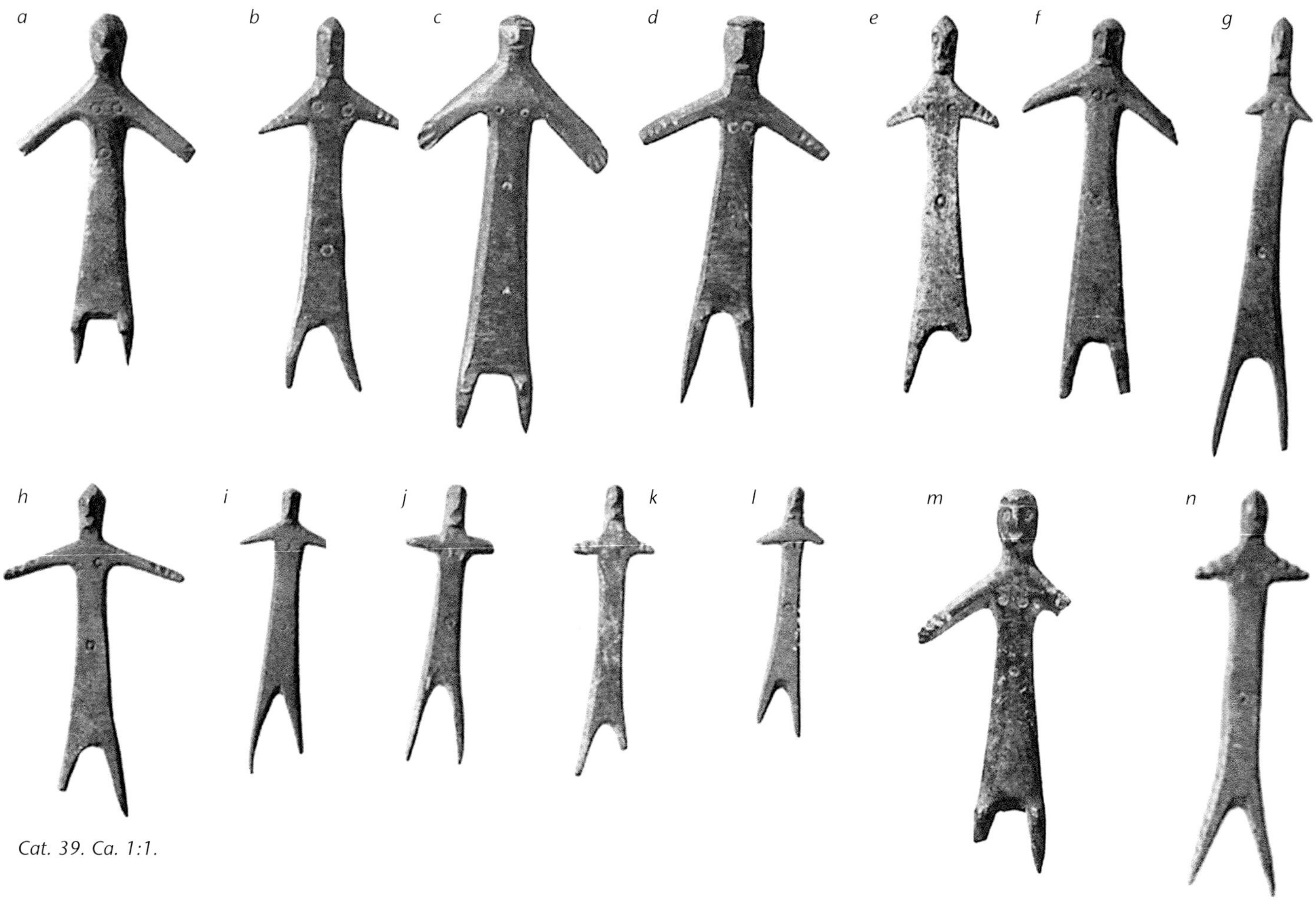

Cat. 39. Ca. 1:1.

CAT. 40. SCHEMATIC FEMALE FIGURE
Inv. no. 4795.
H.: 5,6 cm.
Provenance: Unknown.
Acquisition: 1897. Given by private collector. Originally bought in Rome.
Bibliography: Unpublished.
Technique: Cast. Filing marks. Smooth surface. Light green patina. One leg broken off

Schematic flat figure in long dress. Transversal grooves and incised line at top and bottom of dress.

Cf Cat. 41. Stefani 1935, 158, fig. 3b, votive deposit at Gualdo Tadino.

South Umbrian.
Fourth-Third Century BC.

Cat. 40. Ca. 1:1.

CAT. 41. SCHEMATIC FEMALE FIGURE
Inv. no. 4796.
H.: 5,3 cm.
Provenance: Unknown.
Acquisition: 1897. Given by private collector. Originally bought in Rome.
Bibliography: Unpublished.
Technique: Cast. Partly matt surface. Light green patina. Right arm broken off.

Schematic flat figure in long dress with transversal incisions at lower part. Large cubic head.

Cf Cat. 36; 40. Stefani 1935, 158, fig. 3b, votive deposit at Gualdo Tadino.

South Umbrian.
Fourth-Third Century BC.

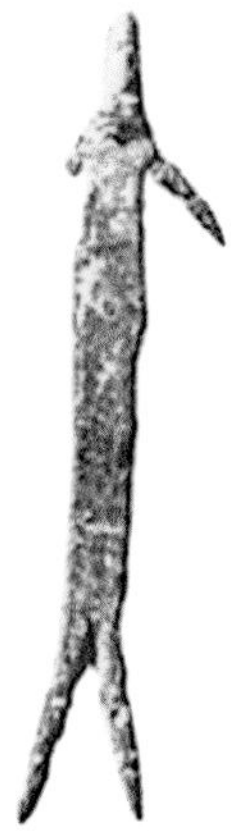

Cat. 41. Ca. 1:1.

COMMENTARY ON SCHEMATIC FIGURINES IN LONG DRESS

These figurines presumably represent females. Parallels in context come from votive deposits found in Umbria and Rome. From Rome there is a find, originally comprizing sixty pieces, of which fourteen came to the Prehistoric Ethnographical Museum in Rome from the Nardoni collection, allegedly found on the Esquiline near the Church of S.Antonio (Colonna 1970, 103).

A terracotta antefix in the shape of a silen's head, found in the votive deposit near the church in 1876/77, indicates the existence of an Archaic temple nearby (Gjerstad 1960, 139 ff., fig. 92,1). The greater part of the deposit was, however, post-Archaic. Several of the pieces in the Danish National Museum are of the "Esquiline"type, and they might even be part of this votive deposit, as they were acquired in Rome at the end of the Nineteenth Century.

Another deposit, coming from a small sanctuary at Gualdo Tadino, points to Umbria as the likely centre of the production of this type of ex-voto. The life of the sanctuary continued into Roman times, as indicated by the pavement of the cella, but the deposit also included eight pieces of *aes rude* (Stefani 1935, 158 fig. 3). The type stretching the arms out obliquely is represented in the Carsòli deposit, which covers the last decades of the Fourth Century BC to 217 BC according to the coin evidence (Cederna 1951, 184). From 1986 to 1990 excavations conducted by the Soprintendenza Archeologica per l'Umbria at Monte Acuto di Umbertide has brought to light a sanctuary with a votive deposit, including approximately 1600 schematic figurines of animals and humans that are very close to the Danish National Museum's flat figurines in chiton. The sanctuary is thought to have been frequented from the end of the Sixth to the beginning of the Fourth Century BC (*Gens Antiquissima Italiae* 1991, 211 ff.). The dating, however, is mainly based on the evidence of the bronzes, and this interesting site does, unfortunately, not contribute to a more precise dating of these votives, that may cover a long period, perhaps beginning in the Fifth Century BC and continuing through the Third Century BC.

Excavations in 1984-85 at Gubbio, Monte Ansciano, have brought to light similar figurines at a site with evidence of ritual practice from the Sixth to the Third Century BC, based on a Sixth Century BC iron fibula and an early Republican moulded coin, again indicating the period attested at Carsòli, *ie* the Fourth to Third Century BC (*StEtr* LIV, 1986, (1988), 379-382.

ATHLETES

CAT. 42. DISCOBOLOS

Inv. no. ABa 707.
H.: 8,9 cm; h. of plinth: 1,8 cm; diam. of plinth: 4,1 cm.
Provenance: Unknown.
Acquisition: 1855/56. Bought in Italy.
Bibliography: Riis 1941, 168 f., note 6. *Idem* 1997, 85 fig. 87.
Technique: Feet and lower part of legs missing. Combined with antique round moulded base with beaded edge, same olive-green patina, but not necessarily belonging. Surface of figure matt and corroded in patches. Olive-green patina.

Cat. 42. Ca. 1:1.

Discobolos, resting on right leg, left leg bent and advanced. Left arm raised, bent at elbow and hand bent back in an Etruscan dancer's gesture. Right lowered hand holds discus facing forwards. Hair arranged in thick roll at neck, leaving ears free. Radiating lines from top of head. Round face with high cheek-bones. Very low forehead. Almond-shaped large eyes, with raised eyelids, iris indicated in middle. Small nose, small smiling mouth with full lips. Figure's right eye placed higher than the left. Face not symmetrical. Faint line around neck indicating chain with round pendant. Breast muscles faintly modelled. Punched circles for nipples and navel. Spinal cleft. The weight on the right leg and the bending of the left free leg does not reflect in the buttocks, which are marked off by a sharp line, but both at the same level. Penis infibulated.

Cf Testa 1989, no. 15, 56-59, crowning piece of candelabrum", likely to have been found at Vulci in 1837). Milani 1905, 241 fig, 41, (Florence inv. 62, said to have come from Castellina in Chianti. Gardiner 1907, 18 fig.7 (Wyndham Cook Collection). de Ridder 1913, pl.13 no.118 (Louvre, from Amykleia). Ny Carlsberg Glyptotek 1928, pl. 95 (H 227). De Agostino 1961, 67 no. 8, fig.7 (from Populonia). Münzen und Medaillen Auktion XXII, 1961 no.72. Mitten-Doeringer 1967, 175, no. 178. Comstock-Vermeule 1971, 164, no. 187. Del Chiaro 1976, pl.57,4 (Ludington Collection, Santa Barbara, California). Hostetter 1986, pl.44 d-f, from Spina tomb 18 (context about 470 BC to later Fifth Century BC.). Maule 1988, pl.24a (Smithsonian Institute, Washington D.C.). Fedeli 1993, 18, fig. 10 (colour).

Gardiner 1930, 154-168 and Thomas 1981, 30 ff. describe the various phases of the discus throw. First the disc is held high in the left hand, then transferred to the right hand, which is lowered behind the body to gain monumentum before the actual throw. The position of the left hand of the Laconian discobolos Louvre 118 (Thomas 1981, pls. X-XI) indicates that the transfer of the disc to the right hand has just taken place. It is also the case with the Boston statuette (Thomas 1981 pl. XII). The still raised left hand might easily be interpreted as a gesture of adoration by the Etruscan artist, as seen for example in the bronze from Populonia (De Agostino 1961, 67 fig. 7). One step further is the transformation into the dancer's gesture which the Copenhagen statuette adopts. The New York discobolos (Thomas pl. XV) still holds discus in the left hand, and so does the Baltimore figurine (Thomas pl. XIV).

Comment

Stylistically the Etruscan discobolos is close to the Laconian athlete Louvre 118, especially remarkable in the head, but also in the emphasis of the pectorals. The gesture of the left hand has either been misunderstood or deliberately transformed into the traditional dancer's gesture, with

Cat. 42. Ca. 1:1.

Cat. 42.

the palm completely upwards and the fingers bent back, seen on many other figurines and in other media like painting or sculpture. It is hardly a gesture of adoration as suggested by Hostetter, unless the gesture in all other cases should also be so interpreted. The gesture with the palm forward of the athlete from Populonia (De Agostino 1961, 67, fig.7), might, however, be that of adoration. The movement of the Laconian discobolos is dynamic, whereas the Etruscan counterpart has been changed into a static position, with the weight on the right leg balancing the raised left arm. Many of the same features are found in the Etruscan piece from the Wyndham F. Cook collection (*JHS* 27, 1907, 18 fig.7). The quiet stance is also characteristic of the Florence bronze (inv.62) from Castellina in Chianti and the very similar piece in Santa Barbara, California, the two of them indubitably from the same workshop, which, however, must be different from the one that produced the Copenhagen piece, whose facial features are different, although the high cheek-bones are predominant in all three bronzes. The face of the Copenhagen discobolos is closer to the standing figure in the Smithsonian Institute. The closest parallel for the stance of ABa 707 is the crowning statuette of the candelabrum from Spina tomb 18 C, thought by Hostetter to be the earliest of the candelabrum figurines. According to this author the earliest bronzes at Spina from about 500 BC are imports from Vulci and later from Orvieto. The standard candelabra from about 480-470 BC are thought to have been cast in the Po valley, probably at Spina.

North Etruscan, Padanian?
Second quarter of Fifth Century BC.

CAT. 43. ATHLETE WITH STRIGILIS

Inv. no. 4982.
H.: 13,3 cm.
Provenance: Northern Italy.
Acquisition: 1900. Bought in London (formerly Coll. Forman).
Bibliography: Riis 1941, 168 note 6.
Technique: Surface matt and corroded in patches. Green patina.

Cat. 43. Ca. 1:1.

Naked athlete with strigilis. Standing on left leg, right leg slightly bent and set to the side, heel free of ground. Left arm held slightly backwards. Pectorals modelled, nipples hollowed out. Spine indicated by groove. Left hip placed higher than right. Fingers indicated. Finely modelled facial features. Raised eyelids. Straight nose and straight mouth, lower lip protruding. Ears placed over hair, which is short, with curls indicated all over.

Cf Testa 1989, no.11, 44-47, crowning piece of candelabrum (second half of Fifth Century BC). List of similar statuettes in Beazley-Magi 1941, II, 176 f. *Etruria Padana* 1960, no. 743 pl.XXV, (beginning of the Fourth Century BC). Bologna City Museum, from the Monte Avigliano necropolis. *Ibid.* no. 777, pl. LIV, "Efebo Fruga", votive deposit, Monte Capra, (about 430 BC.) *ibid.* no. 809, pl. LX, Reggio Emilia Museo Civico, from Servirola S.Polo. Mitten-Doeringer 1967, no. 219, Saint Louis City Art Museum (Fourth Century. BC). Haynes 1985, 202 fig. 134a (420-400 BC).

Comment

The stance and treatment of the body is close to the victorious athlete from Delphi, the style of which is Polycleitan from 460-450 BC. The position of the arms is, however, different. The Vatican candelabrum figurine, Testa 1989 no. 11 has the right hand holding the strigilis behind the nape of the neck, presumably in the process of scraping the back of his shoulder, and the left stretched out at the level of the shoulder. The body is much stockier and the mass of hair fuller. The type of candelabrum belongs to the second half of the Fifth Century BC and is likely to be of Vulcian manufacture.

The Bologna candelabrum crowning piece from Monte Avigliano, *Etruria Padana* no. 743 is an athlete with the arms in the traditional worshipping position. Presumably it belongs to the beginning of the Fourth Century BC.

The statuette from Servirola S. Polo, Etruria Padana no. 809, which is a resting athlete holding the strigilis at his right thigh, left arm akimbo, is also thought to belong to the beginning of the Fourth Century BC. A Felsinian origin is suggested.

The Saint-Louis candelabrum statuette, Mitten/ Doeringer 1967 no. 219 is a discobolus. Both the position of the arms and the stance have affinity to the Copenhagen bronze Cat. 43, which is, however a little earlier.

This bronze also shows affinity to the profile of the head of the athlete from Veii, Sprenger 1972, pls. 12-15, but, again, the torso of this figure is much more modelled and the stance more relaxed, in comparison with the dryness of the treatment of the body of Cat. 43.

The head of the athlete crowning the British Museum candelabrum, Haynes 1985, 202 fig. 134a shares many features with the Copenhagen statuette, whereas the modelling of the torso is more detailed.

An example of a candelabrum with a male crowning figure found in context is provided by the youth severing a lock of his hair, from Spina tomb 1157, Hostetter 1986, pl. 14. This stance is fairly close to that of the Copenhagen bronze. The suggested date of the Spina youth is 450-440 BC, although the contents of the tomb cover a period from the very end of the Fifth and the beginning of the Fourth Century BC. The Copenhagen statuette probably also belongs to the end of the Fifth Century BC, as the facial features point to parallels around 400 BC or after the turn of the Century.

Vulcian.
End of Fifth Century BC.

Cat. 43. Ca. 1:1.

Cat. 43.

SATYRS

CAT. 44. DANCING SATYR

Inv. no. 93.
H.: 9,2 cm.
Provenance: Unknown.
Acquisition: 1867/68. Bought in Paris.
Bibliography: Riis 1941, 122, n.8.
Technique: Smooth surface. Dark green patina with vivid green areas. Missing: tail, front of left hoof, most of right hoof.

Dancing satyr with raised arms, palms open and thumbs extended. Right leg advanced, left set back. Head and upper body tilted backwards. Pectorals and abdomen modelled. Prominent buttocks, left slightly higher. Circular hole for fastening of tail. Legs ending in hooves. Large beard and long moustache with indication of hairs. Small snub-nose, large bulging eyes, low forehead, pointed ears. Hair arranged in fringe and hanging down over shoulders in a smooth mass, finishing in curved line with short oblique strokes.

Cf Gori 1750, 12 f., pl. 7 (Coll. Corazzi). Walters 1899, no. 473 (British Museum), from Chiusi, Neugebauer 1921, 97 f., pl. 53. *Idem* 1936, pl. 27,3-4 (Berlin), from Chiusi.

Comment

Very close to the British Museum satyr from Chiusi, and most likely also from the rim of a coal-burner.

About 500 BC.
Chiusine.

Cat. 44.

Cat. 44. Ca 1:1.

CAT. 45. SATYR
Inv. no. 13341.
H.: 4,6 cm.
Provenance: Unknown.
Acquisition: 1952. Bought from private collector in Copenhagen.
Bibliography; Unpublished.
Tech.; Solid cast. Casting fault under left shoulder. Legs missing from knees. Surface matt, a little pitted. Patina dark brown with buff layer in places.

Cat. 45. Ca 1:1.

Standing satyr with right arm raised, palm forward. Left hand supporting wineskin on shoulder. Trunklike pot-bellied body. Thin thighs. Large head with wrinkled forehead, prominent eyebrows, bulging eyes in deep sockets, small flat nose, moustaches and huge pointed beard covering chest. Upright pointed ears with leaf-pattern. Longish hair radiating from point at crown. Spine indicated. Over buttocks root of tail. Nipples and navel punched. Dotted pattern on wineskin.

Cf Oxford Ashmolean Museum inv. 1924.60, Beazley Gifts 594, pl.77 (ab 500 BC.); Budapest Inv. no. 50,380 (Later part of 5th Century BC).

Comment
Not unlike the Oxford satyr, the position of which was, however, different, perhaps dancing or kneeling. For body, *cf* large bronze Marsyas from Paestum, *EAA* IV, 271, fig. 320, Second Century BC (Colonna).

Fifth Century BC.

BEARDLESS TINIA/JUPITERS

CAT. 46. BEARDLESS TINIA/JUPITER

Inv. no. 4198.
H.: 10,8 cm.
Provenance: Unknown.
Acquisition: 1894. Bought from private collector in Rome.
Bibliography: Salskov Roberts 1993, 294 f., fig.8.
Technique: Matt, smooth surface. Olive-green patina.

Beardless, male figure, standing on right leg, left bent and advanced. Body tilted slightly backwards, right arm raised and wielding the thunderbolt. Left arm with draped cloak extended, hand flat and open.

Large head, short skull with short wavy curls radiating from crown. Low forehead, very large eyes with bulging eyeballs and raised upper lids. Straight nose. Broad mouth with protruding lower lip, corners turned downwards.

Linea alba vaguely indicated. Navel indented. Slight indication of iliac crests. Abdomen slightly curved. Pubic hairs indicated by a row of circles.

Cf Bendinelli 1920, c.238, fig.13, (deposito di Cagli). *BdA* 44, 1959, 316, fig.9. (Chieti Museo Nazionale, without no., from Tornareccio). Chieti inv. 24.501, from Monte Giove, Penna S. Andrea Bentz 1992, pl. 18, fig. 90, Kat. 10,1, likely to come from Telamon.

Latin.
Third to Second Century BC.

Cat. 46. Ca 1:1.

Cat. 46.

CAT. 47. BEARDLESS TINIA/JUPITER

Inv. no. 3242.
H.: 11 cm.
Provenance: Unknown.
Acquisition: 1887. Bought in Napoli.
Bibliography: Salskov Roberts 1993, 294.
Technique: Matt surface. Brownish and green patina.

Cat. 47. Ca. 1:1.

Beardless, standing on right leg, left leg bent and set slightly back. Right arm lowered, hand holding thunderbolt. Left arm raised, hand having clasped now missing object, scepter? Torso bent toward the left, slightly tilted backwards. Small cloak draped over left shoulder. Small head, slightly tilted to the right. Hair radiating from crown and arranged in loose locks forming a roll around forehead and neck. High forehead, vague eyebrows, narrow eyes with raised upper and lower lids. Small nose, lips turned slightly upwards. Broad neck. Torso fully modelled on front and back.

Cf for earlier prototype of Italic beardless Tinia/Jupiter with thunderbolt in right hand: Gori 1750, 9-10, pl.4. = Cortona, Accademia Etrusca inv. 1570 "Jupiter Summanus". Colonna 1970, 27, n. 3, pl. V. Cristofani 1976, 18, figs. 4-5. L'Accademia Etrusca 1985, no. 81, colour pl. p. 66. de Ridder 1913, pl. 27, 312. von Lorentz 1935, pl. 63. *BdA* 1959, 316 fig. 10, Chieti inv. 4948 Bentz 1992, pl. XVIII, fig. 90, Kat. 10,1, likely to be from Telamon.

Comment

The stance of the early prototype is different, the left arm being lowered. The stance of Chieti inv. 4948 is more similar, but the head is more stylized and the body less detailed. The style of the Louvre statuette Cat. 312 is fairly close, but the left arm is akimbo and the thunderbolt larger. The Hellenistic prototype of the figurines is likely to be Lysippos' or Apelles' Alexander, *cf* the statuette from Grado, von Lorentz 1935, pl. 63.

Latin.
Third to Second Century BC.

CAT. 48. BEARDLESS TINIA/JUPITER

Inv. no. 4752.
H.: 16,7 cm.
Provenance: Said to have been found in the Tiber.
Acquisition: 1896. Bought in Rome.
Bibliography: Salskov Roberts. 1993, 294.
Technique: Missing: right foot and ankle, part of scepter. Brown and green patina. Matt, somewhat corroded surface.

Beardless, standing on right leg, the left bent and set slightly back. Right arm lowered and stretched forward, thunderbolt in hand. Left arm raised, holding thin scepter. Folded cloak draped over left shoulder and upper arm. Around head wreath tied at the back. Hair radiating from crown, hanging down in free locks over the nape of the neck and arranged in loose curls over forehead and temples. Head turned to the right. Raised eyelids, irises slightly hollowed out, short nose, full lips, corners turned downwards. Torso front and back richly modelled.

Cf Gori 1750, pl. 8 for style (found near Cortona 1748) Accademia Etrusca 1985, 117, ill. Furtwängler 1903; Furtwängler 1910, pl. 98 n. 463, from Vulci (close). For stance, the Greek bearded Poseidon München Inv. 15 (Coll. Loeb), Ohly, Die Antikensammlungen am Königsplatz, 5th ed., without year, pl. 60. Statuette of Alexander the Great, from Grado (Aquileia), von Lorentz 1935, 333 f., pl. 63. *BdA* 44, 1959, 312, fig.2-4, from Monterazzano, (Viterbo). Bérard-Azzouz 1997, cat. no 31, L'Alexandre d'Agde dit l'Éphèbe.

Comment

The Grado statuette of Alexander is very close as for stance, position of head and drapery, but is holding a sword in his right hand. The prototype for the Etruscan statuettes might well be Alexander holding the thunderbolt by Apelles, *cf* Plutarch, *de Iside et Osiride*, 24; *de fortuna* Alexandri,3.

Second-First Century BC.

Cat. 48. Ca. 1:1.

FEMALE FIGURES. KORE TYPE

CAT. 49. STANDING WOMAN

Inv. no. 133.
H.: 9,2 cm.
Provenance: Unknown.
Acquisition: 1868. Bought in Paris.
Bibliography: Richardson 1983, 305 no. 19.
Technique: Surface smooth. Olive-green patina.

Woman dressed in chiton with sleeves standing on both feet. Left hand holding bunch of folds, right held against side of body. Fingers indicated. Hair arranged in flat roll or fringe with vertical strokes over forehead and mass hanging down neck and shoulders. Large head with strong facial features. Large, almond-shaped eyes, small nose, large full mouth, slightly smiling. Breast modelled, lower body rather flat, but right leg vaguely modelled. Along neckline row of hanging triangles. Folds of chiton indicated by curved lines and dots. On edges of sleeves short, oblique strokes. On feet shoes with rounded toes, no pattern.

Cf for style Florence inv. 254, Bocci Pacini 1984 122, pl. II, c-d, votive deposit at Fonte Veneziana, Arezzo. Also male figures of the same deposit for hair and broad neck, Cristofani 1985, no. 3.1-2. Richardson 1983, 306 no. 24 (Munich 3119). Cristofani 1985, no. 3.15 (Florence 263).

Comment

This figure, described by Richardson as having clumsily modelled features on a head too big for the body, is certainly misplaced in a group called by her "Mannerists" and a subgroup called "Pretty". It fits in much better with the later part of the Fonte Veneziana deposit, with which it shares many features, *eg* hairstyle, proportions between head and body, details of pattern, pose and the fact that only one arm is free of body.

North Etruscan.
About 500 BC.

Cat. 49. Ca. 1:1.

CAT. 50. STANDING WOMAN
Inv. no. 1252.
H.: 9,2 cm.
Provenance: Unknown.
Acquisition: 1878. Given by Mrs. Bech, Valbygaard.
Bibliography: Unpublished.
Technique: Surface corroded. Dark brown and green patina. Under feet tang (modern?).

Woman dressed in sleeved chiton, which she is pulling up with her left hand. Right hand held against side. Breast modelled, lower body nearly flat. Low forehead, large bulging eyes, flat nose, narrow, protruding lips, slightly smiling. Back of skull flat. Hair radiating from crown and coming down over shoulder. Fillet. Elaborate beaded necklace. Border of hanging triangles along neckline of chiton. Broad grooves indicating folds. Low shoes laced on top.

Cf for stance and dress Richardson 1983, pl.. 214, figs.720-721 (Florence 242). Bieber 1915 no. 125, pl. 39. Fogolari 1950-51, 349, fig. 2 (Verona).

North Etruscan.
Beginning of Fifth Century BC.

Cat. 50. Ca. 1:1.

CAT. 51. STANDING WOMAN

Inv. no. ABa 869.
H.: 9,7 cm.
Provenance: Unknown.
Acquisition: 1861. Bequeathed by Th. Reutze, Vienna.
Bibliography: Unpublished.
Technique: Surface smooth. Olive-green patina, rubbed off in parts. Right arm broken off under elbow.

Kore dressed in long tunic with sleeves. Left leg slightly advanced. On head diadem and tall conical tutulus. Breast modelled, lower body rather flat. Left hand large and flat fingers turned backwards. Facial features blurred. Mouth small, smiling, full lips.

Cf Mingazzini 1932, 459 fig. 20, from votive deposit of small sanctuary near Fiesole (close). ABa 869 may well come from the same deposit. *Cf* for tutulus Cristofani 1985, 85 no. 2.12 (Florence Archaeological Museum no. 568).

Northwest Etruscan.
Beginning of Fifth Century BC.

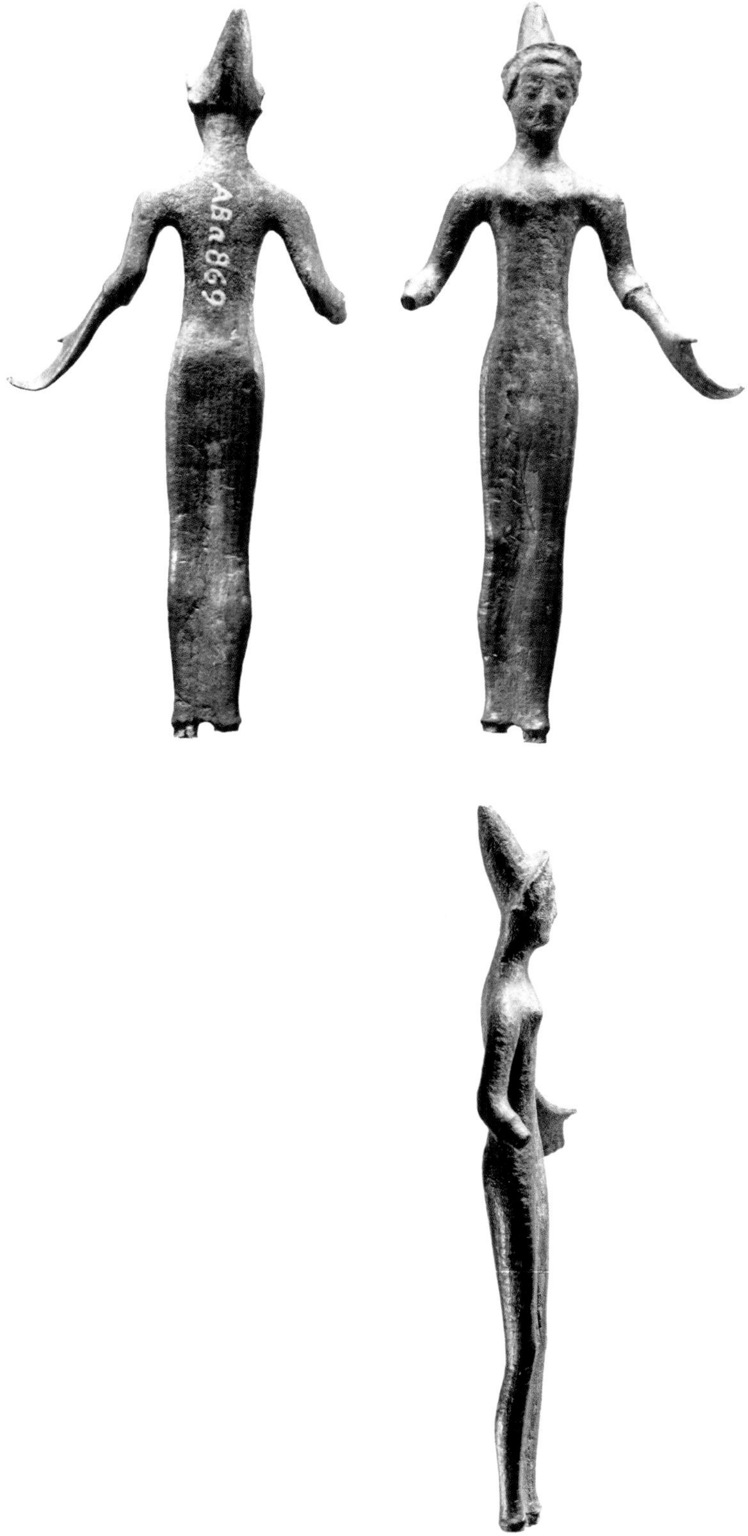

Cat. 51. Ca. 1:1.

CAT. 52. STANDING WOMAN
Without inv. no.
H.: 8,8 cm.
Provenance: Unknown.
Acquisition: Unknown.
Bibliography: Unpublished.
Technique: Surface rather corroded. Dark greenish brown patina. Missing: both arms from under shoulder.

Cat. 52. Ca. 1:1.

Standing kore dressed in long chiton with border of triangles along neckline. Hair arranged in thick roll over forehead, falling down over neck and shoulders in a triangular mass. Large eyes, smiling mouth, prominent chin. Breast and legs vaguely modelled.

Cf Moltesen 1982, 35, fig. 8 (Villa Giulia inv. 6727) from Villa Ruffi, Rimini, About 500-480 BC. Mingazzini 1932, 442-81, esp. 459 ff., figs. 20-23, from sanctuary near Fiesole. Fortuna/Giovannoni 1989, fig. 39, from Lago degli Idoli, Falterona. Cat. 52 may well come from this site.

Northwest Etruscan.
Beginning of Fifth Century BC.

CAT. 53. STANDING WOMAN

Inv. no. 1731.
H. with tang: 9,7 cm. Without tang: 8,5 cm.
Provenance: Unknown.
Acquisition: 1882/83. Bequeathed by V. Freund.
Bibliography: Unpublished.
Technique: Surface smooth. Dark brown patina.
Under feet tang.

Kore holding up chiton in left, now missing, hand. Right arm stretched to the side, fingers turning slightly upwards. Breast modelled, otherwise flat body. On head possibly rounded cap.

Head slightly tilted back. Mass of hair hanging down over shoulders. Low forehead, large obliquely set eyes, small nose, and smiling mouth. Neckline of chiton has border of hanging triangles and punched circles. Also circles and wavy double lines scattered over chiton. Long, pointed shoes with traces of lacing.

Cf Milani 1912 II, pl. 78, (deposit from Broglio, Val di Chiano). de Ridder 1913, pl. 23 no. 236 (Louvre MNC 698). Ny Carlsberg Glyptotek 1928, (H.232), pl. 92, for position, hair and eyes. Maetzke 1957, 495, fig.7, (Chiusi Museum, presumably from near Chiusi, with further references to parallels in the Siena Museum, also likely to come from Chiusi). Richardson 1983, 310, pl. 219, fig. 737 A (Dresden 9596).

North Etruscan, Chiusine?
Beginning of Fifth Century BC.

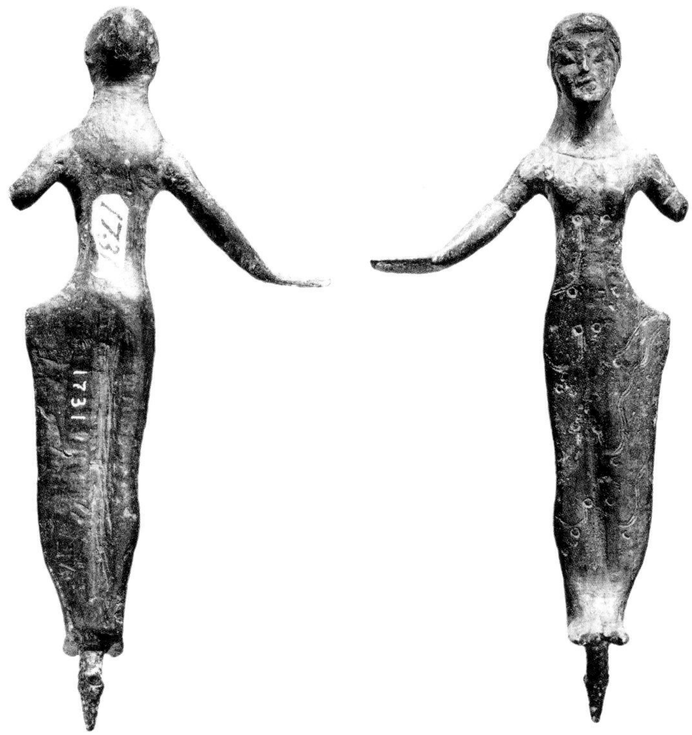

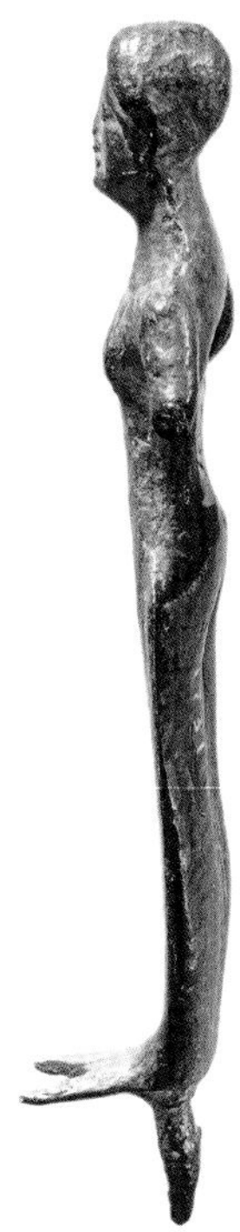

Cat. 53. Ca. 1:1.

CAT. 54. STANDING WOMAN
Inv. no. 116.
H.: 8,5 cm.
Provenance: Unknown.
Acquisition: 1868. Bought in Paris.
Bibliography: Unpublished.
Technique: Solid cast. Fairly smooth surface, with a few corroded areas at the back. Olive-green patina.

Kore standing on both feet, holding round fruit in right hand and grasping a bunch of folds of the chiton with the left. In fact, the hand is placed with the thumb forwards and the four fingers straight on the material at the back, not really grasping it, the hand being in the same position as on figures with arm akimbo. Dressed in long chiton with sleeves to the elbows. Incised lines and tongue pattern along neckline and vertical seam of sleeves. Tall headdress spiralling into a point. Deep lines indicating waist and folds of chiton. Dots between lines, most clearly at back. Breasts modelled, lower body flat. Pointed shoes. Strong regular face, straight eyebrows, almond-shaped eyes. Full, unsmiling lips, small round chin.

Cf Gori 1750, pl. 5. de Ridder 1913, pl. 22,235, the position of the left hand very similar, and so is the tutulus covering the ears. Giglioli 1935, pl. 126,4 (Louvre, from Southern Italy). Thorvaldsens Museum, inv. no. 3. For style of face, *cf* terracotta Poulsen 1949, 19 no. 21, pl. 12, from Taranto (NCGlyptothek I. N. 972).

The facial features point to the Classical period.

Central Etruscan.
460-450 BC.

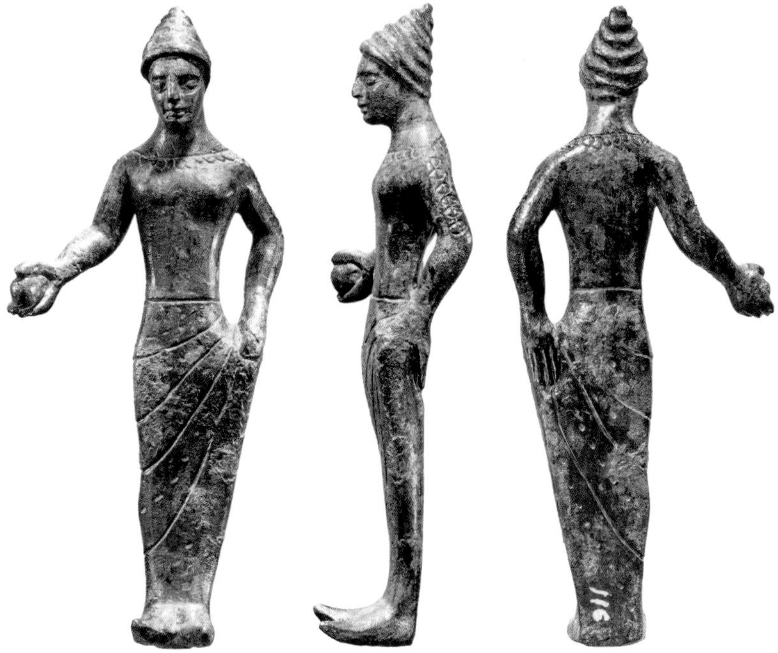

Cat. 54. Ca. 1:1.

Cat. 54.

CAT. 55. STANDING WOMAN

Inv. no. 946.
H.: 13,8 cm.
Provenance: Unknown.
Acquisition: 1876. Bought at Feuardent in Paris.
Bibliography: Riis 1941, 90, note 7, idem 1997, 111, fig. 115, note 265. Richardson 1983, 305 (V 3, Series B Group 3 A no. 20), pl. 217, fig. 729.
Technique: Surface partly smooth, partly a little corroded. Green patina.

Kore holding up sleeved chiton with left hand. Right hand slightly bent at elbow and held along side, but free of body. Breast modelled, body otherwise flat. Eyes triangular, nose small, full smiling lips. Round chin. Hair radiating from crown, and arranged in thick roll over forehead and nape of neck. Ears indicated by grooves in the roll. Round fillet. Flat pointed shoes. On neckline of chiton hanging triangles and circles. Punched circles scattered over chiton. Thin lines indicating folds.

Cf the female of the group, de Ridder 1913 pl. 23, no. 244, (close). Adam 1984 no. 225 for stance, face and incisions on dress (Chiusine, 500-480 BC).

Comment

The rolled-up hair, which is not uncommon in Greek female bronzes, *eg* mirror-supports, is not found in the marble korai, perhaps because these represent young unmarried girls. It is, of course, common in male figurines, Greek and Etruscan. The Acropolis korai cannot be the direct model for this type of Etruscan statuette, which does not wear the Greek himation either. The Etruscan bronze is more likely to represent a married woman wearing the local garment.

Central Etruscan, according to Riis "vulcianizing".
Beginning of Fifth Century BC.

Cat. 55. Ca. 1:1.

CAT. 56. STANDING WOMAN

Inv. no. 4203.
H. with tang: 25 cm. Without tang: 24,1 cm.
W. 2,0202 g.
Provenance: Votive deposit, Villa Ruffi, Rimini.
Acquisition: 1894. Bought in Rome.
Bibliography: Brizio 1890, 208 f. Riis, 1941, 129, pl. 22,3. Messerschmidt 1942, 100. *Willumsen Exhibition* 1947, 42, no. 264. Giglioli 1954, 19 fig. 1 left. Riis 1957, 31 ff., pl. I a-d. Riis 1962, 110, fig. 60. Boethius 1962 figs. 429-432. Monti 1963, 251f. no. 23. Gualandi 1974, 65 no. 101. Sassatelli 1981, no. XXX, 33, 344, figs. 218-220. Moltesen 1982, 36-38, figs. 10-11. *Romagna* 1982, 344 no. 22. Richardson 1983, 279 no. 14, pl. 192 fig. 651. Santuari 1985, 35 f.,1,21. Cristofani 1985, 144 no. 32; 265; Gentili 1985, no. 1.21, 35-36. Romualdi 1987, 302-304, fig. 206. *"Tanagra"*, Exhibition Aarhus 1996, 62, fig. 23. *"Pegasus og Tanagra"*, Exhibition Copenhagen 1997, 43 ff., fig. 30. Rimini Divina 2000, 106 no. 14; Torelli 2000, 622 no. 278. Kunsthallen 2001, Sale catalogue. 10-12 Okt. no. 216, drawing by J. F. Willumsen. Höckmann 2002, 53-58, fig. 72 a-d.
Technique: Solid cast. Bracelet corroded. Otherwise fine, smooth surface. Dark green patina with copper-red areas. Underneath large tang, 1.2 cm, bent and end broken off. Point of right shoe irregular from casting.

Kore standing with left foot slightly advanced, both soles touching the ground. Right arm bent and held closely to the chest, hand grasping now missing object (flower?). Left hand grasping bunch of folds of the chiton, which ends in an elaborate swallow-tail formation spreading over the left foot. Dressed in thin undergarment appearing under sleeves of chiton and over feet, possibly at the neck, with incised pattern; chiton patterned with groups of dots, borders of alternating rectangles and crosses and lined with zig-zags. Over right shoulder Ionian himation with similar borders. On sleeve of right arm indication of buttons and folds. The edges of the sleeves are in relief. Hair arranged in a scalloped fringe, parted in the middle and hanging down in a long mass to the middle of the back, with two thin undulating tresses on each shoulder, one lying in front, the other behind the shoulder and upper arm. Wavy strands of hair at the back are incised. Around head a diadem with incised triangles and dots over forehead. Ears set outside across the diadem. On feet flat shoes with turned-up points and lacing indicated on top. Loose bracelet on left wrist, traces of another on right wrist. Breasts, arm muscles, leg and buttocks modelled. Large, triangular head with low broad forehead and cheeks tapering toward chin. Narrow slanting eyes, with iris indicated by two concentric circles and dots for pupils. Short, straight nose, full lips not meeting at corners, prominent chin.

Cf Walters 1899 no. 497, from Perugia, Lamb 1969, 108, pl. 41c = *EVB*, 314 no. 3. Walters 1899 no. 492, pl. XV = *EVB*, 298, figs. 709-710. Berlin Fr. 2155, from Perugia, *EVB*, 313, figs. 742-743.

Comment

The Rimini kore is unique among archaic Etruscan bronze female statuettes in several respects, such as stance, costume, hairstyle, facial features and use of relief lines or incisions to render hair or material. As for stance, Richardson only has one example of a woman having one arm bent and the lower arm lying across the chest, the hand closed, presumably around an offering, *EVB*, 261, pl. 176, fig. 585, Florence inv. 258, from Arezzo, deposit of Fonte Veneziana (Middle Archaic). Two other statuettes with bent arm have a flat hand pressed against the chest, obviously an entirely different gesture, presumably with a different significance. (*EVB* 263 f., pl. 180, figs. 597-598, Florence inv. 231. *EVB*, 282, pl. 193, figs. 654-655, Arezzo 11.603.The gesture of *EVB*, 281 no. 21, a lost bronze from Marzabotto, only known through a drawing, Reinach II (2), 51, fig. 5, is not quite clear.)

In contrast, the stance with the hand holding an offering in front of the chest is common in the large marble korai from Ionia of the second quarter of the Sixth Century, *eg* the dedication of Cheramyes found in the Samian Heraion, Karakasi 2001, pls. 8-9 (Berlin inv. 1750). In this case the offering is a small hare, *cf op.cit.* pl. 11 no. 9 a. Other devotees offer a bird, *op.cit.* pl. 19 no. 20, Vathy Museum, as do korai from Miletos, *op.cit.* pl. 40, M 4 (Berlin inv. 1791; pl. 46, M 11 (Berlin inv. 1577), and from several other East Greek sites, *eg* the later limestone torso from Klazomenai from the last third of the Sixth Century. (Louvre 3303), *op.cit.* 63, pl. 57.Very few korai from continental Greek adopt this stance, Richter 1968 no. 59, figs. 198-200 considered to be an import from Samos being one example, another the Lyon kore, Richter no. 89, figs. 275-281, also strongly influenced by Ionian art.

The inspiration for the stance of the Rimini kore

Cat. 56. Ca. 80%.

may have come from imports of smaller-size objects like terracotta vases in the shape of a standing woman serving as alabastra, exported from Rhodes, especially for their contents of fragrant oils, to many sites of the Mediterranean in the last quarter of the Sixth Century, *eg* Higgins 1959 no. 49, pl. 10, with hare, excavated at Camiros; no. 57, pl. 13, with dove; no. 110, pl. 21; no. 58, pl. 1 with flower. *Cf* also Richter 1968 no. 146, figs. 462-465. The sizes vary from 23 to 25 cm.

As far as costume is concerned Richardson points out that the small Middle Archaic statuette from the Fonte Veneziana *EVB* fig. 585 is the first to wear the diagonal Ionian himation in the same way as do the women on the aforementioned terracotta alabastra. This garment apparently did not catch on in Etruria until much later, without ever being universally adopted. As Richardson mentions, the artists have often misunderstood the draping of the himation, examples being the large kore in New York, inv. 17.190.2066, *EVB*, 297, pl. 208, fig. 706 or the smaller statuette Volterra 47, *EVB*, 288, pl. 200, figs. 679-681.

A remarkable feature of the himation worn by the Rimini kore is the stylization of the upper folds at the chest under the right hand. They are arranged symmetrically, without taking into account the difference in length due to the diagonal draping of the garment. Also the folds at the back are treated in this way. A parallel to this rather unusual rendering is found on one of the aforementioned terracotta alabastra , Richter 1968, no. 146, figs. 462-465. In larger sculpture this symmetrical arrangement is found on a kore from Paros, Karakasi, *op.cit.* pl. 80a-b and on the Lyon kore Karakasi, pl. 132, which shares the broad shoulders and muscular upper arm with the Rimini kore.

The chiton with a pattern of incised groups of dots can be found in Tarquinian painting on a dancer in the Tomba delle Leonesse from about 530 BC (Sprenger/Bartoloni 1977, pl. 87.

The laced-up shoes with turned-up points worn by the Rimini kore seem to be generally accepted from the the second quarter of the Sixth Century BC, whereas the Greek korai have bare or sandalled feet.

The Rimini kore has two thin undulating locks coming down over either shoulder, one in front of the shoulder, the other behind, but separated from the central mass of hair falling over the back, where the single strands are incised. In Middle Archaic Etruscan bronzes tresses are rare, one example being the kore Bibliothèque Nationale 204, *EVB*, 265, pl. 182, fig. 605, which has two substantial tresses over each shoulder, framing the breast. In Late Archaic occasionally a single lock falls on either shoulder, eg *EVB*, 296, pl. 207, fig. 705 (Berlin 7316). Apart from this eccentric statuette, classified as "Latin" by Richardson, the Rimini kore seems alone in having adopted this hairstyle.

The hair over the low forehead appears in a scalloped fringe, which becomes common among Etruscan bronze statuettes in the last decade of the Sixth and the first decade of the Fifth Century, although not combined with tresses, *eg EVB*, 284, pl. 195, figs. 660-662. *EVB*, 285, pl. 196, fig. 668. *EVB*, 295, pl. 207, figs. 701-703.

Greek marble korai, starting with the Lyon kore from after the middle of the Sixth Century, have a scalloped fringe, usually combined with three or more tresses on either side and a mass of hair hanging down the back, *eg* Karakasi, pl. 132; pl. 133; pl. 166; pl. 257; pl. 267; pl. 268.

In Etruscan terracotta sculpture a maenad antefix at the Portonaccio temple at Veii, from the end of the Sixth Century, offers a remarkable example of a scalloped fringe, which, however, is not combined with tresses, (Banti 1965, pl. 48).

In wall-painting a dancer from the Tarquinian Tomba dei Giocolieri illustrates very well the hairstyle of the Rimini kore, having a scalloped fringe and one lock of hair over the front of the shoulder and another behind the back of it, most likely showing the common fashion around 520 BC. (Sprenger/Bartoloni 1977, pl. 93).

The facial features of the Rimini kore do not reveal any close relationship with other Etruscan statuettes. The head is large with a triangular face, a broad low forehead, narrow slanting eyes and a prominent chin. These characteristics are found in Ionian art, *eg* in a marble head from Miletos (Richter 1968 no. 95, figs. 293-295). This style may have come to Etruria through small imported artefacts like the ivory figurine from Ephesos, Richter *op.cit.* no. 81, figs. 259-262. The slanting eyes become widespread with the Ionian influence on the art of several Etruscan areas, *eg* found in terracotta sculpture on the Sarcophagus degli Sposi (Sprenger/Bartoloni 1977, pls. 114-115) or in repoussé works like the Loeb tripod from Marciano near Perugia, *ibidem* pl. 103.

The large cast statuette Berlin Fr. 2155 from Perugia (EVB, 313, figs. 742-743) has some facial features in common with the Rimini kore, *eg* the slanting eyes, the

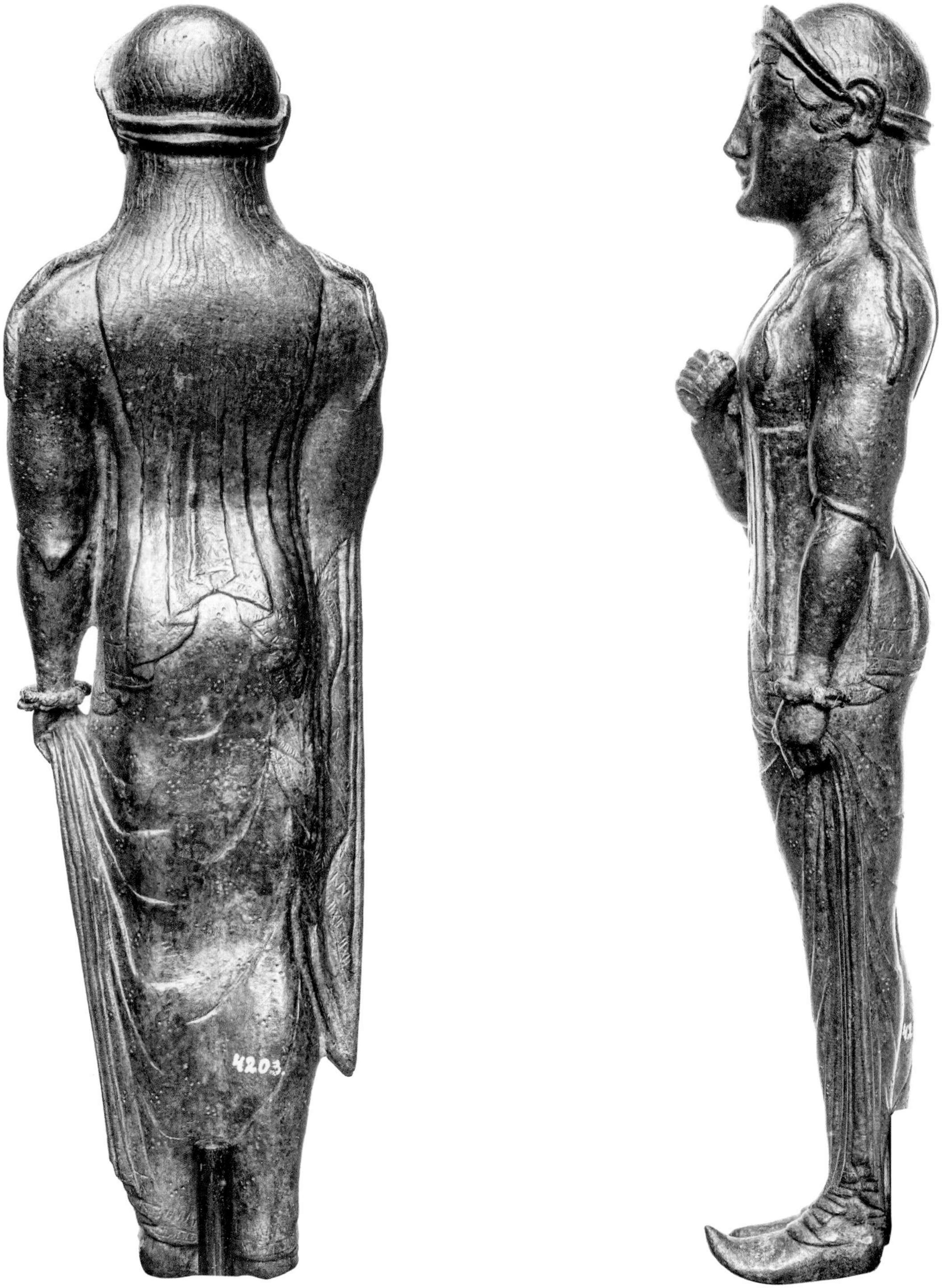

Cat. 56. Ca. 80%.

low forehead, the prominent chin and the general structure of the head, but without really looking like her, and the concept of the nearly flat body of the Berlin figure is quite different from the muscular arms and the modelled buttocks and legs of the Copenhagen statuette, which – without any followers either – remains unique among the Etruscan Archaic bronzes.

The artist creating her may have been a migrant bronze caster getting a commission from a patron, perhaps himself a foreigner in the area, but who specifically asked for a statuette adopting the Ionian stance with the hand holding an offering in front of the chest, although this was not the common ritual practice in the local sanctuaries.
Northeast Etruscan.
Last decades of the Sixth and first decade of the Fifth Century BC.

Cat. 57. Ca. 1:1.

CAT. 57. STANDING WOMAN
Inv. no. 615.
H.: 10 cm.
Provenance: Unknown.
Acquisition: 1871/82. Bought in Naples.
Bibliography: Unpublished.
Technique: Surface partly smooth, partly, especially at back, pitted and corroded. Olive-green patina.

Woman standing on both feet. Left hand grasping bunch of folds, the right, very large hand, held out to the side, palm forward. Hair short, with roll or fringe over forehead, and diadem. Low forehead, large bulging eyes, the right one placed lower than the left. Short nose, upper lip protruding, strong, round chin. Body very flat. Breasts not modelled. Deep lines indicate necklace with pendants and folds of chiton. Two rows of punched circles along sleeves and more scattered over especially the upper part of the chiton.

Cf de Ridder 1913, 238, pl. 23 For head, Giglioli 1954, 22, fig. 4, from Villa Ruffi, Rimini (Villa Giulia 6727) The folds of the lower part of the chiton, as well as the interest in patterns, recall the Rimini kore, Cat. no. 56.

Northeast Etruscan.
Early Fifth Century BC

CAT. 58. STANDING WOMAN

Inv. no. 4976.
H.: 13,3 cm.
Provenance: Viterbo.
Acquisition: 1900. Bought from Simonetti in Rome.
Bibliography: Riis 1941, 92, no. 7, pl. 18,4.
Technique: Surface partly smooth with corroded areas. Olive-green patina with a few reddish spots. Under the feet traces of tangs.

Woman standing on right leg, the left slightly bent. Both feet fully touching the ground, but left hip placed higher than the right. Dressed in sleeved chiton and large cloak draped over left shoulder and lower body. Left hand grasping some material of the cloak. Right hand has a cylindrical perforation for now missing object. Over right shoulder a ribbon or strap. Low, slightly pointed shoes, upper curved edge indicated. Hair divided in the middle and arranged in roll over forehead and nape of neck, leaving ears free. Strands of hair indicated by grooves. Raised eye-lids, small, straight nose, full, unsmiling lips, small chin, under feet traces of tangs.

Cf for style Milani 1912 II, pl. 87, (statue in *pietra fetida* from Chianciano). Also head in *pietra fetida* from Chiusi, Chiusi, Arch. Museum inv. 3016, Prima Italia 1981, 161 no. 107. For type and position Mitten-Doeringer 1967, 169, no. 168, (Fogg Art Museum). For face, Giglioli 1935, pl. CCCXXIX,4, antefix from Tarquinia. For face, Hostetter 1986, pl. 19b-20, Spina no. 16, female crowning statuette of candelabrum, tomb 136 A (About 400 BC). Adam 1984, no. 234.

Cat. 58. Ca. 1:1.

Comment

Although there are several parallels to Chiusine sculpture, Vulci is perhaps the more likely place for quality production in this period.

Vulci.
430-400 BC.

Cat. 58.

CAT. 59. HEAD OF WOMAN

Inv. no. ABa 165.
H. with tang: 4 cm. Without tang: 3,5 cm.
Provenance: Unknown.
Acquisition: Bought in 1828.
Bibliography: Unpublished.
Technique: Matt, corroded surface. Dark brown patina with a few green areas.

Head of woman with substantial tang for insertion. Facial features rather vague. Almond-shaped eyes, upper lid indicated by two lines, small straight nose, small mouth, corners turned down. Hair parted in middle and arranged in wavy mass to each side, rolled up at the back into broad, but flat chignon and held by broad ribbon. On crown wavy lines from parting.

Cf for hairstyle, Adam 1984 no. 234. For style, male votive head, h.3,3 cm, from Ghiaccia Forte, north of Marsiliana d'Albegna, found in building A in a settlement active from about mid-Fifth Century BC to the beginning of the Third Century BC, Del Chiaro 1973, 350, pl. 60, fig. 5. 1974, 389, pl. 77 fig. 11.

Central Etruscan.
Late Classical.

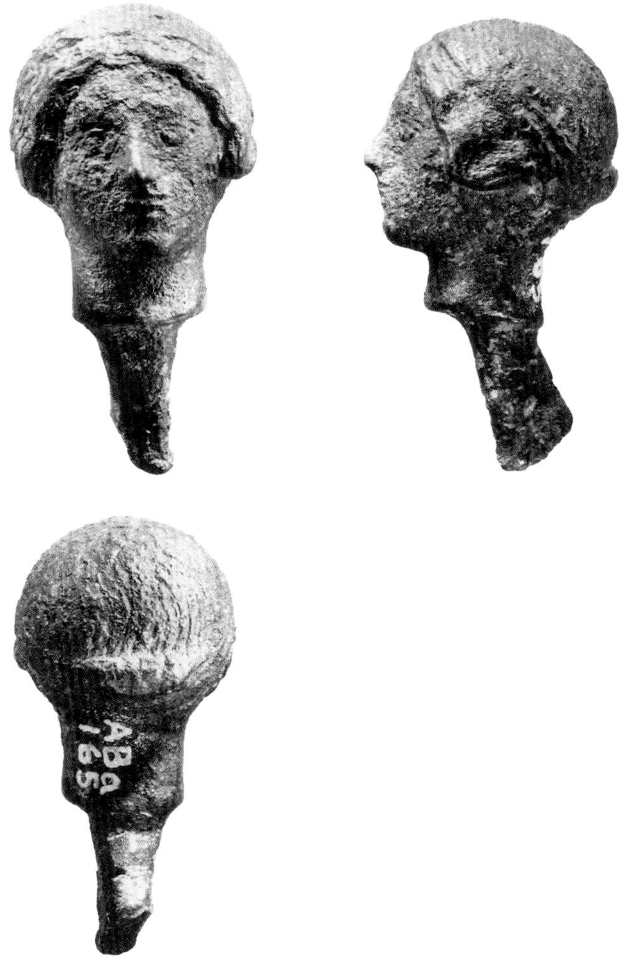

Cat. 59. Slightly enlarged.

Cat. 60. Ca. 1:1.

CAT. 60. STANDING WOMAN
Inv. no. 5368.
H. with base: 11,4 cm. Base: 3,5 X 2,3 cm.
Provenance:" Rome or"environs".
Acquisition: 1903. Bought in Rome.
Bibliography: Riis 1941, 61 f., pl. 10,4. Richardson 1983, 286 no. 3.
Technique: Surface smooth in parts. Bluish green patina with lighter spots on shoulders.

Woman standing on flat, rectangular base. Figure tilted forward. Right arm bent and stretched forward, thumb, index and middle finger holding conical fruit, two fingers bent. Left arm not free of body, hand grasping bunch of folds of chiton. Dressed in long, sleeved chiton. Flat, slightly pointed shoes, laced on top. Chiton has zig-zag and dot border at neckline. Along sleeves vertical line bordered with dots. Around head upright diadem with zig-zag pattern, leaving ears free. Hair arranged in thick roll over forehead, with a mass hanging down to middle back. Strands of hair incised. Small pointed face, faint eyebrows, large eyes, small nose, unsmiling mouth, pointed chin. Broad shoulders, breasts, legs and buttocks modelled. Left buttock higher than the right one.

Cf bronze lebes, in Chiusi, with seven figurines attached to rim. Hus 1975, pl. 31. *StEtr* IV, 1930, pl. 28,6, 361 (Kestner-Museum, Hanover).

South Etruscan.
First quarter of Fifth Century BC.

CAT. 61. STANDING WOMAN

Inv. no. ABa 167.
H.: 6,7 cm.
Provenance: Unknown.
Acquisition: Bought in Florence before 1830.
Bibliography: Unpublished.
Technique: Surface partly smooth, with corroded area at legs. Olive-green patina. Round indentation on forehead, damaged area on right side of top of head. Corrosion at nose, mouth and chin. Lead under feet from fixing into plinth. Perforation between feet. The left hand held mirror, presumably a later addition, which has now been removed.

Cat. 61. Ca. 1:1.

Woman dressed in long chiton with sleeves to the elbows. Standing on both feet which are turned outwards. Pointed shoes with criss-cross lacing. Right hand, open, resting against thigh. Breasts modelled, figure otherwise flat. Eyes indicated by punched circles with centres for pupils set in very large sockets. Mouth indicated by broad oblique furrow. Hair parted in middle and falling down in long mass, finishing in oval line. Straight strands of hair incised. Fillet.

Cf Cristofani 1985, no. 2.10, from Brolio (Florence 571).

Comment

Cat. 61 may fit into the late-ionizing production, of which there are several examples in the Brolio deposit.

North Etruscan.
End of Sixth or Beginning of Fifth Century BC?

GODDESS

CAT. 62. HEAD OF MATER MATUTA

Inv. no. 4798.
H.: 3,5 cm.
Provenance: Unknown.
Acquisition: 1897. Given by private collector. Originally bought in Rome.
Bibliography: Unpublished.
Technique: Surface matt. Light green patina. The neck ends in broad flat tang for insertion (into plinth?). Filing marks.

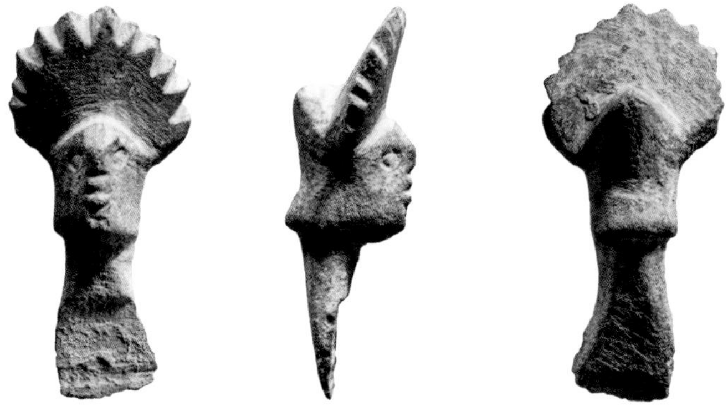

Cat. 62. Slightly enlarged.

Head of woman with large flat semi-oval headdress with eleven indentations along edge. Head cubic with pointed crown.Short hair ending in rounded edge at the nape of the neck. No forehead, punched circles for eyes. Short nose, full lips.

Cf for headdress Richardson 1983, 21 f., pl. 7 figs. 28; 29, pl. 228 fig. 764 = Adam 1984 no. 250 (Bibl.Nat. 212).

The tall headdress is not very common, but is found on a few early bronzes in the votive deposit at Satricum, which was found inside and in front of the foundations of the earliest temple, covering a period from the early 7th to the middle of the 6th Century BC. Richardson, (*EVB*, 23) suggests that this feature may have been borrowed from a Phoenician Astarte type.The divinity of the sanctuary is identified by epigraphical evidence as being Mater Matuta.

This head is quite close to that of the large statuette of a striding female in the Bibliothèque Nationale no. 212. The head Cat. no. 61 was presumably meant to be inserted into a plinth by itself, representing the goddess Mater Matuta as *pars pro toto*.

On Mater Matuta, Livy 6,33,4: 28,11,2. Lucretius V 656-657; Nonius Marcellus, *de proprietate sermonum* I, p 66,9 ed. Lindsay 1903, p.92, including a reference to Cicero, *Tusc.* I (28). The ancient authors agree that Mater Matuta is a goddess of the early morning light and that she is identical to the Greek Leukothea.

Latin.
Sixth to Fifth Century BC?

FEMALE WORSHIPPERS

CAT. 63. WOMAN WITH PATERA

Inv. no. 5362.
H.: 8,5 cm.
Provenance: Villa Shada at Castiglione del Lago.
Acquisition: 1902/3. Bought in Florence.
Bibliography: Unpublished.
Technique: Bluish green patina. Under feet a rectangular block of lead for fixing the statuette into a plinth.

Cat. 63. Ca. 1:1.

Flat statuette of woman holding a patera in right advanced hand and a flat box (acerra) in the left, which appears under the cloak. She is dressed in a chiton with a belt placed just under the breasts and a cloak covering the back of the head and the lower body. The feet appear under the chiton. On the head, which is turned to the right, a diadem with three protrusions. The hair is divided in the middle. The face is triangular with very large obliquely set eyes, irises hollowed out. Oblique strokes, triangles and dots decorate borders of chiton and cloak. On patera and box incised cross and dots.

Cf Gàbrici 1906, c. 237, fig. 46, (Bolsena, Scavi nel sacellum della Dea Nortia sul Pozzarello), Arch.Mus. Florence. Also examples in Naples, 1.c. note 1. Riis 1941, 124 (beginning of Fourth Century BC). Cederna 1951, 169 ff. (Carsòli). Haynes 1960, pls. 15,1; 18,6-9 (Nemi Second Century BC). Lebel 1961, pl. XLVL,4. Fleischer, 1967, pl. 115,226. Colonna 1976-77, 47, pl. 1, nos. 4.-5. Ammirati, Bronzetti votivi etruschi e italici nelle Civiche Gallerie di Arti Antica,"Musei Ferraresi", 9-10, 1979-80, (13-53). M.T. Amorelli, I materiali archeologici preromani del Museo Oliveriano di Pesaro, Roma 1982. Santuari 1985, 152,8,1 B 5 (Punta della Vipera). Cristofani 1985, 24; 276 no. 77. Bentz 1992, pl. 30, fig. 165, Kat. 22,1.6, likely to come from near Siena. Caravale 2003, nos. 98, 99, 101.

The type is known from sanctuaries at Bolsena, Carsòli, Nemi and Punta della Vipera, but especially interesting are the statuettes with identical inscriptions dedicating them to the goddess Cel, found in a votive deposit, near Lago di Trasimeno. Around 1928 they were part of a private collection in Castiglione del Lago and were published by Colonna in 1976-77.

The examples from Carsòli are dated by coins to the period between the last decades of the Fourth Century BC and 217 BC, the year of the introduction of the *riduzione unciale*, the coins of which are not represented at this site.

North or Central Etruscan.
Third to Second Century BC.

CAT. 64. CLOAKED WOMAN

Inv. no. 1257 c.
H.: 6,3 cm.
Provenance: Unknown.
Acquisition: 1878/79. Given by Mrs. Bech, Valbygaard.
Bibliography: Unpublished.
Technique: Matt surface. Greenish and brown patina. Lower part of right arm and hand missing.

Flat woman dressed in chiton, with belt placed high under breasts and cloak fastened on head and coming down over left shoulder. On the back the cloak hangs from the wreath and covers the body. Right arm extended to the side. Left arm, appearing from under the cloak.

Cf Cat. 63 (inv. no. 5362). Cat. 65 (inv. no. 1257 b).

Central Etruscan.
Third to Second Century BC.

Cat. 64. Ca. 1:1.

CAT. 65. WOMAN WITH INCENSE BOX

Inv. no. 1257 b.
H.: 7,5 cm.
Provenance: Unknown.
Acquisition: 1878/79. Given by Mrs. Bech, Valbygaard.
Bibliography: Unpublished.
Technique: Surface corroded. Brown patina. Central tang. Right arm broken off over elbow.

Flat woman holding incense box in left hand appearing from under cloak. Right arm has originally been advanced. Dressed in chiton with belt under breasts and cloak draped over left arm. Headdress with three ornaments. Facial features very blurred.

Cf Cat. 63 (inv. 5362). Cat. 66 (inv. no. 4797). Adam 1984 no. 326. Caravale 2003 no. 106.

Central Etruscan.
Third to Second Century BC.

Cat. 65. Ca. 1:1.

CAT. 66. WOMAN WITH PATERA

Inv. no. 4797.
H.: 4,8 cm.
Provenance: Unknown.
Acquisition: 1897. Bought in Rome.
Bibliography: Unpublished.
Technique: Surface matt, but even. Green patina. Central tang.

Cat. 66. Ca. 1:1.

Flat worshipper holding patera in advanced right hand. Rudimentary left hand appearing from under cloak, indicated by furrow over left shoulder. On upper body five dots. On head four-leaved wreath. Large, bulging eyeballs, irises shallow. Small mouth, lips curved downwards. The back is completely flat.

Cf Cat. 63 (inv. 5.362). For type Oxford Museum no. 1230.872. Lebel 1961, pl. XLVI,5. Monacchi 1988, pl. 38 d, votive deposit of Grotta Bella (Terni) (very close). Bentz 1992, pl. 44, fig. 252, Kat. 33,5.5, likely to come from near Perugia.

Umbrian.
Third to Second Century BC.

CAT. 67. WOMAN WITH PATERA

Inv. no. 1734.
H. with tang: 8,6 cm. Without tang: 8,2 cm.
Provenance: Unknown.
Acquisition: 1882/83. Bequeathed by V.Freund.
Bibliography: Unpublished.
Technique: Surface slightly matt and corroded in parts. Dark brownish-green patina. Central tang, partly broken off. Filing marks at back.

Cat. 67. Ca. 1:1.

Flat female worshipper holding patera in advanced right hand. Rudimentary left hand appearing from under cloak draped over left shoulder and arm. Dressed in chiton with belt placed high up. Diadem with six leaves. Hair parted in the middle on crown and appearing under diadem over forehead. Large eyes, smiling mouth.

Cf Cat. 63 (inv. 5362). Bentz 1992, pl. XXX, figs.166-169, Kat. 22.

North or Central Etruscan.
Third to Second Century BC.

CAT. 68. WOMAN WITH PATERA
Inv. no. ABa 874.
H.: with tangs: 12,6 cm. Without tangs: 11,6 cm.
Provenance: unknown.
Acquisition: 1860/61. Bequeathed by Th.Reutze, Vienna.
Bibliography: Unpublished.
Technique: Surface matt and corroded. Brown and green patina. Under feet broad flat tangs. Between them lead soldering.

Female worshipper dressed in a long chiton with patterned belt placed under breasts. Cloak covering head and left shoulder and draped around hips. Left hand appearing on hip, right hand stretched forward holding patera. Large head, plastic eyeballs with irises hollowed out, snub-nose, full lips, corners turned downwards. Hair arranged in roll over forehead, surmounted by diadem with spiral pattern. Figure hollow at the back.

Cf Ghirardini 1888, 89 no. 49, pl. VIII,7, from fondo Baratela, Este. de Ridder 1913 pl. 28, no. 316. Richter 1915 no. 177 ff. Gàbrici 1906, c. 238, fig. 46, (Bolsena, sacellum della Dea Nortia sul Pozzarello). Bentz 1992, pl. XXIX, fig. 20,2,3, possibly from near Siena.

North Etruscan.
Third to Second Century BC.

Cat. 68. Ca. 1:1.

Cat. 69. Ca. 1:1.

Cat. 69 A. Ca. 1:1.

CAT. 69. CLOAKED WOMAN
Without inv. no.
H. without tang: 8,9 cm. With tang: 9,6 cm.
Provenance: Unknown.
Acquisition: Unknown.
Bibliography: Unpublished.
Technique: Surface matt and corroded. Brown and green patina. Large central tang under feet.

Woman dressed in tunic, with belt placed under breasts, and long cloak covering head and draped over lower body and left arm. Right arm extended. Hand broken off. Left hand, lumplike, showing under folds of cloak. Figure flat at the back.

Cf Cat. 68 (ABa 874). Bentz 1992, pl. IX, fig. 42, Kat. 4.1, from sanctuary at Fiesole; pl. XIV, figs. 68-69, Kat.8.9, from Radicofano.

North Etruscan.
Third to Second Century BC

CAT. 69 A. CLOAKED WOMAN
Inv. no. ABa 578.
H.: 9,8 cm.
Provenance: Unknown.
Acquisition: 1853/54. Bought from private collector.
Bibliography: Unpublished.
Technique: Surface matt. Dark-brown patina. Missing: Right hand and left foot. Under right foot short tang.

Flat statuette of woman, hollow at the back. She stands on the right leg, the left leg being bent. Dressed in a chiton with belt placed just under the breasts and cloak covering head and draped round hips and lower body. Right hand stretched forward, presumably having held a patera. No details of face.

Cf Bentz 1992, pl. IX fig. 42, Kat. 4.1 and figs. 43-44, Kat. 4.2, both from sanctuary at Fiesole (health aspects); pl. XIV, figs. 68-69, Kat. 8.9 and figs. 70-71, Kat. 8.11, both from Radicofani; pl. XXIV, figs. 124-125, Kat.15.1.1.

North or Central Etruscan.
Possibly Third Century BC.

CAT. 70. CLOAKED WOMAN
Inv. no. 1257 a (1257 = eleven pieces).
H.: 7,5 cm.
Provenance: Unknown.
Acquisition: 1878-79. Given by Mrs. Bech, Valbygaard.
Bibliography: Unpublished.
Technique: Smooth surface. Reddish-brown patina.
Right arm broken off over elbow.

Flat figure with large cloak draped over left shoulder and arm. Right arm stretched to the side. Left hand appears from under cloak. Large head with very sketchy indication of eyes and mouth. Horizontal furrow indicating hairline. Hair arranged in bonnet at the back. Folds of cloak indicated by broad furrows.

Cf Cat. 71 (Inv. no. 1.910). Reinach 1897, II, p. 610,6 (Louvre 670) Maetzke 1957, 498, fig. 12, Chiusi Museum no. 4032. Andrén 1967, pl. XXXII c, from Sanctuary at Cannicella, Orvieto (quite close). Caravale 2003 no. 133.

Central Etruscan.
Second Century BC.

Cat. 70. Ca. 1:1.

CAT. 71. WOMAN HOLDING ROUND FRUIT
Inv. no. 1910.
H.: without tang: 6,9 cm. With tang: 7,8 cm.
Provenance: Unknown.
Acquisition: 1882/83. Bought in Tarquinia.
Bibliography: Unpublished.
Technique: Matt corroded surface. Brown and green patina.
Under feet bifurcate tang.

Flat cloaked figure (woman?) holding round fruit (pomegranate?) in advanced right hand. Left hand, open, also advanced. Dressed in tunic with short sleeve and cloak draped over left shoulder. Hair seems to be parted in middle and arranged in roll. On crown concave headdress.

Cf Cat. 73 (inv. 1257 b). For prototype, de Ridder 1913, pl. 26, 293. Richardson 1953, 116, fig. 28. Andrén 1967, pl. XXXII b, from sanctuary at Cannicella, Orvieto no. 38. Del Chiaro 1973, pl. 60 fig. 1, from Ghiaccio Forte near Grosseto. Cristofani 1985, 169 no. 63. Caravale 2003 no. 88.

North Etruscan.
Fourth to Third Century BC or later.

Cat. 71. Ca. 1:1.

MALE WORSHIPPERS

CAT. 72. STANDING MAN WITH PATERA AND INCENSE BOX

Inv. no. 5369.
H. without tang: 11,1 cm.
Provenance: Perugia.
Acquisition: 1903. Bought in Rome.
Bibliography: Unpublished.
Technique: Fine, smooth surface. Grey patina. Under feet corroded bits of tangs. Filing marks at back.

Standing man holding patera in right hand stretched to the side and incense box (akerra) in left advanced hand. Standing on right leg, left leg set a little back. Dressed in cloak draped over left shoulder and reaching below the knees. On head large wreath with six leaves. Hair arranged in large locks framing face. Furrows indicate hair on crown and under wreath at back. Collar bone and pectoral modelled. Small face with large eyes, irises hollowed out, lower lids marked, full, slightly open lips, dimple in small chin. The figure is flat at the back, but folds of cloak modelled. Fingers and toes indicated. Radiating strokes over patera and box.

Cf Gàbrici, 1906, c. 234, fig. 45, (Bolsena sacellum della Dea Nortia sul Pozzarello). de Ridder 1913, pl. 27, 307 (close). Bieber 1915, 70 no. 215, pl. XLIV. Royal Scottish Museum, Edinburgh, 1957.514. Budapest no. 66.124. A, 61.124 A, Debrecen Mus. Et.IV,13. Mazzolai 1958, fig. 16, Grosseto Museum, several pieces. Maetzke 1957, 499, fig. 18, Chiusi Museum no. 2213. Menzel 1960, pl. 30, 24. Haynes 1960, pls. 16-17. (Nemi, Second Century BC.), with list of priests and priestesses. Adam 1984, 203 nos. 318-219, with further examples. Monacchi 1988, 88 f., pl. XXXVIII, d-e, stipe votive di Grotta Bella (Terni). Bentz 1992, 58 ff., pl. XII, upper row, from Orvieto, Second Century BC. Caravale 2003 nos. 115-120.

Central Italy.
Third to Second Century BC.

Cat. 72. Ca. 1:1.

Cat. 73. Ca. 1:1.

Cat. 74. Ca. 1:1.

CAT. 73. STANDING MAN
Inv. no. 1257b (11 pieces)
H.: 6,2 cm.
Provenance: Unknown.
Acquisition: 1878-79. Given by Mrs. Bech, Valbygaard.
Bibliography: Unpublished.
Technique: Brown patina. Smooth surface.

Flat male worshipper dressed in cloak draped over left shoulder and arm. Left open hand appearing from under cloak. Right hand advanced, palm upwards. Hair indicated by rows of short strokes radiating from crown. Punched circles for nipples and navel.

Cf Reinach II, 610,6 (Louvre 670). de Ridder 1913, pl. 26 no. 293. Maetzke 1957, 498, fig. 12, Chiusi Museum o. 4032. Andrén 1967, pl. XXXII c, from sanctuary at Cannicella, Orvieto (quite close). Del Chiaro 1973, pl. 60, fig. 3 (female) found at Ghiaccio Forte near Grosseto. Cristofani 1985, 169 no. 63. Bentz 1992, pl. XLI, fig. 231. Kat. 31.2.3 (Cortona 1634), from Cortona or surroundings. Caravale 2003, nos. 84-85.

North or Central Etruscan.
Third Century BC.

CAT. 74. STANDING MAN HOLDING INCENSE BOX
Inv. no. ABa 247.
H.: 6,7 cm.
Provenance: Unknown.
Acquisition: 1825. From the collection of the Archbishop of Taranto.
Bibliography: Unpublished.
Technique: Surface matt and corroded. Dark brown and green patina. Missing: right arm from elbow.

Male worshipper holding round object flattened at top (akerra?) in advanced left hand. Right arm lowered. Standing on right leg, left set a little back. Dressed in cloak draped over left shoulder. Hair radiating from crown. Large, bulging eyes, very pronounced eyebrows and forehead, large mouth and chin.

Cf inv Cat.73 (inv. 1257 b). Cat. 74 (inv. ABa 247). Santuari 1985, 31 no. 1.9, Florence inv. 141, from Paterno di Vallombrosa (Arezzo) man holding exta in left hand, with dedicatory inscription, *TLE* 685: *eit viscri ture/arnθ pumpuś*. Bentz 1992, pl. XXXIX, fig. 222, Kat. 30,2,2 (Siena 3), with inscription *:zla/pa*, from Siena or surrounddings.

Central or North Etruscan.
Second half of Third Century BC.

Cat. 75. Ca. 1:1.

Cat. 76. Ca. 1:1.

CAT. 75. STANDING MAN HOLDING INCENSE BOX
Inv. no. 1257 d.
H.: with tangs: 8,9 cm. Without tangs: 8,5 cm.
Provenance: Unknown.
Acquisition: 1878/79. Given by Mrs. Bech, Valbygaard.
Bibliography: Unpublished.
Technique: Surface matt and corroded. Brown patina. Lump shaped tangs under feet. Missing: Head and right hand.

Male worshippper dressed in cloak draped over left shoulder. Advanced left hand holding flat box. Right arm a little raised and stretched forward. Figure flat, caving in, hollow at the back.

Cf Cat. 74 (ABa 247). Reinach 1904 III, p. 144,10. (Rouen). Cederna 1951, 191 fig. 8,7, votive deposit, Carsòli). Santuari 1985, 31 no. 1.9 (Florence 141, with Etruscan dedicatory inscription, TLE 685: *eit viscri ture/ arnθ pumpuś* (from Paterno di Vallombrosa (Arezzo) = Bentz 1992, pl. XL, fig. 226, Kat. 30,3,3.

North Etruscan.
Second half of Third Century BC.

CAT. 76. STANDING FIGURE
Inv. no. 1257e.
H.: 5,2 cm.
Provenance: Unknown
Acquisition: 1878/79. Given by Mrs. Bech, Valbygaard.
Bibliography: Unpublished.
Technique: Corroded surface. Light green patina.

Flat figure (woman?) dressed in chiton and cloak draped over left shoulder. Right arm bent and stretched to the side, hand open. Left hand appearing from under cloak. Folds of material indicated by grooves front and back. Low forehead, large eyes, short nose. Hair radiating from crown and arranged in roll all around.

Cf Gàbrici 1906, 202, fig. 27 (Bolsena, sacellum della dea Nortia sul Pozzarello), covering a period from Third Century BC to Third Century AD. Budapest Inv. no. 51841. Florence no. 91390. Andrén 1967, pl. XXXII c, Sanctuary at Cannicella, Orvieto. Bentz 1992, 30, Kat. N. 3, pl. VI, figs. 25-26, from surroundings of Siena. Caravale 2003 no. 90.

Central Etruscan.
Prototype Fourth Century BC, but this piece indubitably later, Third Century BC?

CAT. 77. NAKED MAN. LEFT ARM AKIMBO
Inv. no. 1251c.
H. with tang: 7,2 cm. Without tang; 6,4 cm.
Provenance: Unknown.
Acquisition: 1878/79. Given by Mrs. Bech, Valbygaard.
Bibliography: Unpublished.
Technique: Surface uneven and pitted. Greenish brown patina. Missing: right arm from under shoulder. Under feet short central tang.

Cat. 77. Ca. 1:1.

Naked man standing on left leg, right leg slightly bent and set to the side. Left arm akimbo, right lowered. Nipples and navel indicated by dots, *linea alba* by furrow, genitals modelled. Head long and large. Marked oblique eyebrows, obliquely set eyes, outer corner lower than inner. Hair arranged in roll around head, surmounted by cap.

Cf Fogolari 1950-51, pl. I bottom row (no. 21). For stance, Romualdi 1984, pl. I (Arezzo), from second half of fourth to third Century BC. Bentz 1992, pl. 36, fig. 198, Kat. 27.1.1, from Cortona; pl. 36, fig. 199, Kat. 27.1.2, possibly from Fiesole. Caravale 2003 no. 92.

North Etruscan.
Third Century BC.

CAT. 78. NAKED MAN. LEFT ARM AKIMBO
Inv. no. ABa 579.
H.: 6,8 cm.
Provenance: Unknown.
Acquisition: 1853/54. Bought from private collector.
Bibliography: Unpublished.
Technique: Dark green patina with brown crust and verdigris patches. Missing: Right leg broken off at mid-thigh.

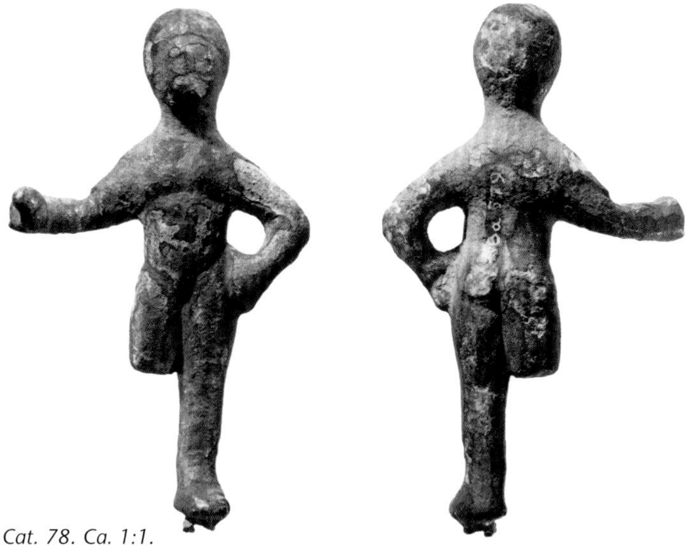
Cat. 78. Ca. 1:1.

Naked man standing on left leg. Left arm akimbo. Right arm bent at elbow and held forward. Cylindrical perforation in right hand for object. Facial features blurred. Left buttock higher than right. Muscles of torso modelled.

Cf Cat. 77 (Inv. no. 1251 c). Fogolari 1950-51, pl. I, bottom row (no. 21), Chieti 3291. Chieti 4371, from Carsoli, NS 1951. Bentz 1992, 108, pl. 33, fig. 181, Kat. 24.6.

North Etruscan.
Third Century BC.

CAT. 79. NAKED MAN

Inv. no. 11350.
H.: without tang: 7,0 cm. With tang: 7,4 cm.
Provenance: Said to be from Pompeii.
Acquisition: 1942. Bought from private collector.
Bibliography: Unpublished.
Technique: Surface matt, somewhat corroded. Dark and light-green patina, with brown areas on the legs. Under feet a flat lump of metal from casting funnel, used for fixing into base.

Cat. 79. Ca. 1:1.

Beardless naked youth standing on left leg, right leg slightly bent. Right arm stretched to the side, palm forward. Left hand, with short cloak draped over lower arm, has a cylindrical perforation for now missing object. Hair short, divided at the back by a line, from which emanate horizontal, slightly oblique grooves. Narrow forehead continuing into nose which merges into mouth and chin. Oblique eyebrows, protruding eyeballs. The torso vaguely modelled.

Cf Riis 1941 pl. 21,2. For type De Ridder 1913 pl. 26,293. Mazzolai 1958, p. 219, fig. 34 a-c, Grosseto. Bentz 1992, 27, pl. V, figs. 16-17, Kat. I,4 (Sovana).

North Etruscan.
Third Century BC.

CAT. 80. STANDING MALE
Inv. no. 13397.
H.: 7,2 cm.
Provenance: Said to be from Pompeii.
Acquisition: 1953. Bought from private. (Formerly Coll. Forsberg, Sweden, 1899).
Bibliography: Unpublished.
Technique: Surface fairly smooth. Olive-green patina. Under feet notched broad tang.

Naked, beardless male standing on right leg, left slightly bent at knee, but legs not separated. Left arm akimbo, right resting against upper thigh. A cloak is possibly covering the back of the legs. The front of the torso is vaguely modelled. The face is small and triangular. Large round eyes, otherwise featureless. The hair is arranged in a roll over forehead and coming down into a triangle at the back.

Cf Romualdi 1984, 469 f., pl. I b; (Arezzo Arch.Mus. 11.838); pls. I c, II a-b (Florence Arch. Mus. 211), from surroundings of Arezzo, (close). Bentz 1992, 108 f., pl. 33, fig. 183, Kat. 25.1.1

Cat. 80. Ca. 1:1.

Comment

A specimen of a fairly small series of worshippers, ascribed by Romualdi to an Aretine production covering a period from the second half of the Fourth Century BC to the Third Century BC. It is suggested by Romualdi that the type is connected with a local cult of Dionysos.

North Etruscan.
Third Century BC.

FIGURES OF HERAKLES

INTRODUCTORY NOTE TO CAT. 81-91 (HERAKLES WITH LION HELMET)

In Archaic Greek art the predominant Herakles type seems to have been a figure in dynamic forward movement, with the lion-mask covering the head and the skin hanging from the outstretched left arm, while the hero clasps a bow and the right hand brandishes the club at a level with the hero's head. Evidence is found in vase-painting, *eg* the Euphronios krater in Arezzo (inv. 1465, *ARV*[2], 15 no. 6) or a Corinthian cup with black outline drawing in Athens (NM 409, *LIMC* IV, no. 1096).

This combination of stance and attributes is seen in numerous Herakles statuettes found in Italic votive deposits, but an important difference is, however, that the Italic Herakles is beardless, while the Greek Archaic hero usually is bearded.

A rare early example of a Greek beardless Herakles is the kneeling archer of the Aigina pediment (Ohly 1976, pls. 30-35). Another is the head in Berlin (Furtwängler 1895, 82, fig. 32) both bearing witness to the existence of a youthful Herakles type in the first half of the Fifth Century BC in Greece, but the bearded type seems to have become predominant, in vase-painting as well as in sculpture, from Archaic times onwards.

In Cyprus a beardless type with lion-helmet is known in limestone sculpture throughout the Fifth Century BC and on coins from the Fourth Century BC (Salskov Roberts 2002, 85, note 16). This may be a Cypriot version of the hero influenced by the iconography of Melquart, but may, of course, refer to sculpture from the Greek Mainland. Many of the great sculptors of the Classical period are credited with having made their version of Herakles. Cicero refers in passing to Polykleitos having made a Herakles with lion-skin (Cic. de orat. II,69), but no identification with extant copies remains undisputed, and whether it was bearded or not is an open question.

Certain Polykleitan features can, however, be noticed in some of the small-scale Italic production, *eg* in the large statuette Louvre 283 (De Ridder 1913, pl. 25) from the Abruzzi, in a Herakles from the Paelignan area, Sulmona inv. 4567, Papi 1991 no. 1 fig. 1 and in a statuette in the Museo Irpino, Avellino, inv. 808 (Papi 1991, no. 5, figs. 5-6, which is so close to Cat. 81 (ABa 48) as to suggest that it is the work of the same artist, especially because of the details of the lion-skin. Papi suggests a date for this production in the last decades of the Fifth and the beginning of the Fourth Century BC because of the close connection with the Polykleitan tradition. This may be true for the fine Bibliothèque Nationale inv. 536 (Adam 1984 no. 289:, Papi 1991 no. 4, fig. 4), but the more modest examples are more likely to represent this tradition continuing through the Fourth Century and later in the Sabellian area. *eg* the round facial features of Cat. 82 (ABa 221) are not very classical. The profile of Cat. 83 (ABa 219) is close to coins featuring Alexander wearing the lion-helmet, minted in Tarentum in 315 BC. The slender proportions of Cat. 84 (ABa 223) also point to a later Lysippean tradition. Lysippos is known to have made two statues of Herakles for Tarentum, but again, from what ancient authors tell us about them, these particular works cannot be the prototypes for the lion-helmeted attacking Herakles (Strabo VI,278; Suida s.v. Basilica)

Cat. 84 (ABa 223) is closely connected with a fine example in Florence (inv. 146, Richardson 1964, fig.XLVIIa) and a statuette coming from S. Giovanni in Galdo, where a small Italic sanctuary is situated (Di Niro 1977, 38 f.). Di Niro points to the Lysippean features of this type, which is fairly common in Samnium. Several scholars who also see Pergamene influence in this production, put it as late as the mid-Second Century BC (Richardson 1964, 161; Colonna 1971, 176). This is obviously true for examples like Chieti nos. 835 and 838 from the Caramanico deposit (Papi 1992, 139 nos. 2 and 3) and Chieti 2393 from Bucchiano, to which can be joined Cat. 85 (ABa 49) as coming from the same workshop. Characteristics are the dance-like twist of the body and the hairstyle with rows of voluminous curls. The Caramanico deposit covers a wide chronological range, and it is hardly possible to date the lion-helmeted Herakles as such. It seems to have its ultimate inspiration in Archaic Greek art, but the Italic version is shaped in the Fourth Century BC and remained flourishing, at any rate quantitatively, for several centuries, right down to the Social War and, after that, continuing into Roman times, when there was still a demand for Herakles statuettes at the many small local sanctuaries.

Cat. 87 (ABa 222), the surface of which is rather corroded, has some details in common with Cat. 81 (ABa 48) and Cat. 84 (ABa 223), but the proportions, with a fairly large head, may connect it with Colonna's Group"Bologna" with a more Etruscan orientation.

Cat. 88 (ABa 231) belongs to the type of Cat. 81 and 84, and the crude Cat. 89 (3762) is also a remote descendant of that tradition.

Cat. 90 (ABa 236) also finds parallels in the Caramanico deposit, but comes from a workshop different from that of Cat. 84 (ABa 223) and Cat. 85 (ABa 49).

Cat. 86 (ABa 47), which has some affinity to Cat. 90 (ABa 236) as far as proportions are concerned, has a very detailed modelling of the torso in the Hellenistic tradition, reminiscent of the "Resting Herakles" from Sulmona, which is now convincingly considered a product of the school of Lysippos, working in Italy from the reductions made by the master (Moreno 1995, 103), but the treatment of the head of Cat. 86 with round eyes, small nose and mouth does, however, point to a late phase of that tradition.

Although Cat. 91 (ABa 220) has the lion-helmet and shows the same stance as the previous statuettes, it belongs to a rather different school. It also presents the variation of holding the apple of the Hesperids in the outstretched left hand. The proportions are very different, the head being very large and the torso very short. The few parallels also come from different sites, *eg* the temple of Aphrodite at Erice. The quality is quite good, and perhaps this statuette is earlier than the previous ones and closer to Greek artistic tradition.

Cat. 81. Ca. 1:1

CAT. 81. HERAKLES WITH LION-HELMET
Inv. no. ABa 48.
H.: 10,3 cm.
Provenance: Unknown.
Acquisition: 1813 in the Royal Danish Kunstkammer.
Bibl. Unpublished.
Technique: Smooth surface. Black patina. Left lower arm and right foot missing. Two modern perforations on left foot.

Herakles standing on right leg, left bent and set to the side. Right arm bent and raised, the hand with a cylindrical perforation having held the weapon, now missing. Lion-skin covering head and draped over left arm. It is notched along edges and has a herring-bone pattern down the middle. Triangular eyes with raised lids, vague eyebrows, low forehead continuing straight into nose. Broad lips, corners turned slightly downwards. Torso well-modelled. Pubic hairs notched.

Cf Walters 1899, nos. 1245; 1262. Florence, Mus.Arch. 146, publ. Richardson 1964, fig. XLVIIa. de Ridder 1913, pl. 25, (Louvre 283. Prov. Abruzzi). Di Niro 1978, pl. X a-b, Campobasso inv. 1014, from Vinchiaturo (close). Adam 1984, no. 293. Papi 1989, fig. 28, Chieti inv. 4567, from Sulmona, sanctuary of Herakles Curinus, very close, same workshop, same artist. For stylization of lion-skin, Papi 1991, 1062, no. 5, figs. 5-6, Avellino, Mus. Irpino inv. 808.

Sabellian.
Prototype Fourth Century BC, but examples continue into Late Hellenistic Times.

Cat. 82. Ca. 1:1

CAT. 82. BEARDLESS HERAKLES BRANDISHING CLUB, WITH LION-SKIN OVER HEAD AND LEFT ARM

Inv. no. ABa 221.
H.: 11,6 cm.
Provenance: Unknown.
Acquisition: 1825. With the collection of the Archbishop of Taranto.
Bibliography: Unpublished.
Technique: Surface smooth in parts. Dark green to black patina.
Missing: Right hand and both feet.

Herakles standing on right leg, left leg bent and set forward. Right arm raised, left arm stretched forward, hand grasping now missing object. Head inclined toward left shoulder. Lion-skin over head, paws knotted at neck, back draped over left arm. Herring-bone pattern along middle of lion-skin, the edges of which are notched. Muscles of torso modelled, iliac crest indicated. Eyes large, eyelids raised. Small snub-nose, small full mouth.

Cf de Ridder 1913, pl. 25 (Louvre 283) rather close as for lion-helmet and notched edges of lion-skin and structure of face. Lebel 1961, pl.XXXIX,2. Mitten-Doeringer 1967, 179 no. 183. Menzel 1966, pl. 27,58.; Papi, 1991, 128 no. 1, 139 fig. 1, Chieti 834, from Caramanico, position close, lion-skin wrapped slightly differently, generally quite close. Papi 1989, 84, fig. 29 Sulmona, Mus. Civico, face close. Chieti 1453, from Villa S. Maria, very close, also face. Fishbone pattern on the back of lion-skin. Di Niro 1978, pl. XIII, Campebasso inv. 1009, from Talvento, close. Biella 2015, I.b.1, pl. XX, c-d, from sanctuario di Corfinio.

Sabellian.
Obviously Classical inspiration, but also Late Hellenistic features.
Second half of Second Century BC.

Cat. 83.

Cat. 83. Ca. 1:1.

CAT. 83. HERAKLES WITH LION-HELMET
Inv. no. ABa 219.
H.: 15 cm.
Provenance: Unknown.
Acquisition: 1825. With the Collection of the Archbishop of Taranto.
Bibliography: Salskov Roberts 2002, 84 f., figs. 3-4.
Technique: Surface smooth. Upper layer of surface corroded in some areas on legs. Pitted on left shoulder and lion-skin on lower arm. Olive-green patina. Left foot modern.

Beardless Herakles standing on right leg with the left advanced. Right arm raised, cylindrical perforation for missing weapon in hand. Lion-skin covering head, and draped over left advanced arm, paws tied in front of chest. Plastic herring-bone mid-rib along back of skin. Left hand clasps object (bow?) now missing. Head of lion modelled.

The head of Herakles has a low forehead, vague brows, large eyes with plastic lids, small short nose, very full, half opened lips, firm chin. Torso well modelled, iliac crest indicated, pubic hairs plastic. Right hip higher than the left. Knee-caps and calves modelled.

Cf Reinach III, 69,8, Coll. Loeb. Mitten-Doeringer 1967, 179 no. 183, Kansas City, close. van Wonterghem 1973, pl. VI, fig. 7, Sulmona Mus. Civico, close. Di Niro 1978, pl. XIII, Campebasso inv. 1009, from Talvento, quite close. Adam 1984 nos. 289-290.

Comment

Cat. 83 has a stouter build, with Polycletan reminiscenses, than the specimens in Kansas City and the Bibliothèque Nationale, which are also more upright, whereas Cat 83 leans forward in a dynamic movement, more like the Sulmona Herakles, who is, however, more slender.

Sabellian.

Prototype end of Fourth Century BC. The profile of the face close to coins of Alexander wearing the lion-helmet, minted in Tarentum in 315 BC. Colonna 1971, 176 f., followed by Adam 1984, dates several of the parallels in the second half of the Second Century BC and later.

CAT. 84. HERAKLES WITH LION-HELMET
Inv. no. ABa 223.
H.: 11,9 cm.
Provenance: Unknown.
Acquisition: 1825. With the collection of the Archbishop of Taranto.
Bibliography: Unpublished.
Technique: Smooth surface. Right front foot missing.

Cat. 84. Ca. 1:1.

Herakles standing on right leg, left foot advanced. Right arm bent and raised, having held now missing weapon. Left arm lowered, hand holding apple. Lion-skin decorated with alternating rows of stamped circles and short oblique strokes, covering head and draped over left arm. Low forehead, vague eyebrows, large almond-shaped eyes with raised upper lids, short, straight nose, sharply cut lips curving downwards, small, firm chin. Back of head flat. Slender finely modelled torso tilted towards the left. Nipples indicated by punched circles. Long legs with modelled knees and calves.

Cf Walters 1899, nos. 1245, 1262. Richardson, 1964, fig. XLVIIa, Florence Arch.Mus. 146, close. Lebel 1961 pl. XXXIX,2. Mitten-Doeringer 1967, 179, no. 183. Reinach, IV, 123,5. van Wonterghem 1973, pl. VI, fig. 7, Sulmona, Mus. Civico. Palermo. Di Stefano no. 47, Chieti 1453 from Villa S. Maria, close, esp. stance.

Comment

Di Niro 1977 no. 11, pl.XII from S. Giovanni in Galdo, very close (same artist?). The lower jaws of the lion-helmet reflect the raised cheekpieces of a proper warrior's helmet, *eg* statuette BM 456, *EVB* pl. 129, fig. 437, or of the helmet used by Minervas like Florence 70793, *EVB*, pl. 247, fig. 825, etc. Biella 2015, I.a.1, pl. I a-b Santuario di Corfinio.

Cf for face BM 455 Giglioli *AE*, pl. 221, 1, also Florence 586 Giglioli *AE*, pl. 221,2 = Cristofani 1985, no. 87.

The body of Florence 146 is very close. It is placed by Richardson in a mid-Second Century BC context. The stance and proportions of Cat. 84 are Lysippean, but the face may show even older features, as the affinity to the warrior Florence 586 indicates.

The Herakles from S. Giovanni in Galdo is so close, also in the cold-work of the lion-skin, as to suggest the same workshop, perhaps even the same artist. It also shares the uncommon feature of the left hand holding one of the apples of the Hesperids.

It is likely to be the product of an eclectic classisistic workshop capable of producing good quality statuettes. Biella 2015, 70f. is prone to look for parallels from the Third Century BC. In note 19 she refers to the hairstyle of the Montecchio figure, Cristofani 1985, no. 71, which, however, is dated to the Second Century BC by Richardson, *AJA* 62, 1958, 344 and Haynes 1960, 43 f.

Sabellian.
Late Hellenistic Period.

CAT. 85. HERAKLES WITH LION-HELMET
Inv. no. ABa 49.
H.: 9,7 cm
Provenance: Unknown.
Acquisition: Before 1813 in the Royal Danish Kunstkammer. Bought on West auction, Spengler, 68.
Bibliography: Unpublished.
Technique: Surface matt, but even. A few chips on back. Dark green and black surface. Missing: Right hand with club, left forefoot and end of lion-skin.

Cat. 85. Ca. 1:1.

Beardless Herakles with head covered by lion-helmet and back of lion-skin wrapped round left arm, which is bent at the elbow and held forward. Paws tied in front. Ears and mane plastically indicated. Right arm raised, brandishing now missing club. Standing on right leg, left leg set back in a dancelike movement. Head turned to the left. Hair parted in middle and arranged in rows of curls parallel to parting. Very large almond-shaped eyes, small nose, full lips surrounded by vertical lines, small chin.

Cf Papi, 1991 139 nos. 2-3, Chieti 838; 835, from Caramanico, very close, same workshop; also Chieti 834, Papi *l.c.* no. 1, ill. Prima Italia 1981, 205, no. 148. Colonna 1971, 176, Chieti 2393, from Bucchianico, very close, same workshop. Di Stefano 1975 no. 49, pl. XV, Palermo. Biella 2015, I.a.52, pl. XIV, a-b from Santuario di Corfinio.

Sabellian.
On date, *cf* Colonna 1971, 176: about 150-90 BC.

CAT. 86. HERAKLES WITH LION-HELMET
Inv. no. ABa 47.
H.: 10,7 cm.
Provenance: Unknown.
Acquisition: In the Royal Danish Kunstkammer before 1813.
Bibliography: Unpublished.
Technique: Surface smooth in a few areas, otherwise rather corroded. Dark, greyish-green patina. In left foot a plaster filling.

Beardless Herakles with lion-skin over head and left arm. End of skin reaches left leg, middle part missing. Paws tied in front. Standing on right leg, left leg set back, only toe touching ground. Right leg missing from middle thigh. Right arm lowered, broken off over elbow. Front and back of torso modelled in great detail. The belly is pushed forward and the iliac crest accentuated. Head small. Features very vague. Round eyes, small nose, small mouth. Short strokes at lion-skin at back.
Cf Adam 1984, no. 296, Herakles resting right hand on club. Biella 2015, 30; 76, I.b.1, pl. XX c-d, from Santuario di Corfinio.

Sabellian.
150-100 BC, based on prototype of "resting Hercules" from the Fourth Century BC.

Cat. 86. Ca. 1:1.

CAT. 87. HERAKLES WITH LION-HELMET
Inv. no. ABa 222.
H.: 9,4 cm.
Provenance: Unknown.
Acquisition: 1825. From the collection of the Archbishop of Taranto.
Bibliography: Unpublished.
Technique: Surface corroded. Green patina. Missing: club, bow, both feet.

Beardless Herakles holding now missing club in raised right hand. Lion-skin over head and draped over left arm. Paws tied in front. Left hand grasping object (bow?), now broken off. Triangles and dots along back of lion-skin. Standing on right leg, left advanced. Right buttock much higher than left. Long modelled torso. Large head, large eyes, aquiline nose; broad smiling mouth.

Cf Colonna 1970, pl. 139, no. 563. (Group "Bologna"). Di Niro 1978, pl. XIII, Campobasso inv. 1019. Papi, 1991, 139, fig. 2, Chieti 838, from Caramanico.

Sabellian.
Fourth Century BC.

Cat. 87. Ca. 1:1.

CAT. 88. HERAKLES WITH LION-HELMET

Inv. no. ABa 231
H.: 8,3 cm.
Acquisition: Unknown.
Provenance: 1825. From the collection of the Archbishop of Taranto.
Bibliography: Unpublished.
Technique: Surface matt, but fairly even. Dark green to black patina. Missing: Right arm from under shoulder, left hand, left leg from under knee.

Beardless Herakles with head covered by lion-helmet and lion-skin hanging from left outstretched arm. Standing on right leg, left bent and advanced. Right arm raised. Vague indication of paws tied in front. Vague herringbone pattern on back of lion-skin. Oval face, very vague features. Slight indication of iliac crest.

Cf Walters 1899, no. 1245, Colonna 1971, 176, pl. 27, fig. 10 (Group "Caramanico").

Sabellian.
150-90 BC.

Cat. 88.

CAT. 89. HERAKLES WITH LION-HELMET
Inv. no. 3762.
H. with club; 16,2 cm.
Provenance: Unknown.
Acquisition: 1891. Bought in Rome.
Bibliography: Unpublished.
Technique: Surface smooth in parts, with some brown crust and some corrosion, Light vivid green patina.

Herakles standing on right leg, left leg bent and set forward. Right arm raised, wielding club. Left arm lowered, hand open, palm forward. Lion-skin covering head and draped over left arm, paws tied in front of chest. Face very crude, no forehead, short, prominent nose, raised irises set in angular frames. Large vaguely defined mouth. Vaguely modelled torso, navel indicated by circle.

Cf Walters 1899, no. 1262. *Italia Settentrionale* 1964, pl. 80, 164, no. 320, Gretta votive deposit (Trieste). Guida/Loseri 1978, 43, no. 28, from Adria (?). Tagliamonte 1994, pl. IV b, from temple of Aphrodite, Erice.

Sabellian.
Second half of Second to the beginning of the First Century BC.

Cat. 89.

CAT. 90. HERAKLES WITH LION-HELMET

Inv. no. ABa 236.
H.: 7,4 cm.
Provenance: Unknown.
Acquisition: 1825. From the collection of the Archbishop of Taranto.
Bibliography: Unpublished.
Technique: Matt surface. Dark brown patina. Missing: Right leg from middle thigh, left leg from over knee. Both hands.

Cat. 90. Ca. 1:1.

Beardless Herakles with lion-skin over head, paws tied in front, the rest draped over left arm. Right arm bent and raised, brandishing now missing weapon. Large head with vague facial features. Lion mask indicated on top and back of head. Vague facial features.

Cf Maiuri 1926, 250 fig. 3, left and centre, from votive deposit, Sepino (ancient Altilia). Di Niro 1978, pl. XI, Campobasso, inv. 1014 from Vinchiaturo; Papi, 1992, 129 nos. 5 and 6, Chieti 840, Chieti 836, both from Caramanico.

Comment

The votive deposit from Sepino is likely to antedate the destruction of the town in 293 BC by the Romans, but the type seems to continue into the late Hellenistic period.

Sabellian.
End of Fourth Century BC.

CAT. 91. HERAKLES WITH LION-HELMET
Inv. no. ABa 220.
H.: 10 cm.
Provenance: Unknown.
Acquisition: 1825. From the collection of the Archbishop of Taranto.
Bibliography: Unpublished.
Technique: Surface smooth. Dark green patina.

Beardless Herakles with lion-skin over head and left arm. Brandishing weapon, now missing, in raised right hand. Standing on right leg, left bent and set forward. Right buttock much higher than left. In left hand apple. Paws of lion-skin not indicated. Full lion-mask seen from above on top of head. Herring-bone pattern on back of skin. Lower end of thorax vaguely modelled. Head large, completely flat at back. Large almond-shaped eyes, outer corners tapering into a point. Small, short nose, very full lips, round chin.

Cf Colonna 1970, pl. 117, nos. 475, from Volturara Appula; 476 (Karlsruhe). Boucher 1970, Lyon I no. 79 (close). *LIMC* IV, 2, 478 no. 498 (Madrid). Palermo 8170 (B 144, coll Astuto), Di Stefano 1975 no. 45 pl, XI. Di Niro 1978, pl. XI, Campobasso inv. 1014, from Vinchiaturo. Adam 1984 no. 287, for proportions and lion-head. Tagliamonte 1994, pl.IVc, from temple of Aphrodite, Erice.

For proportions, stance (legs reversed) and central excrescence of lion-head cf Cristofani 1985, 121 no. 7.4, Herakles from Villa Cassarini, Bologna, also holding apples, thought by Cristofani to be from a Paduan workshop under Greek influence, Polykleitan derivation, about 400 BC.

Sabellian.
End of Fifth Century BC to the beginning of the Fourth Century BC.

Cat. 91. Ca. 1:1.

INTRODUCTORY NOTE TO CAT. 92-103

A bareheaded Herakles brandishing his weapon in his raised right hand in a dynamic movement, while the lion-skin sweeps backwards from the lowered left arm, is represented by several statuettes in the collection.

Two of these statuettes, cat. 92 and 93 fit into Colonna's group"Sulmona" and are possibly works by the Maestro C. Two others belong to the closely connected group Baranello, one, Cat. 99, possibly being by the Maestro B. The workshop should most likely be found in the Central Italic area. The ultimate inspiration for this type is indubitably Italiote sculpture of the Fourth Century BC, as represented in vase-painting on an Apulian bell-krater by the Eton-Nika Painter from about 370 BC (British Museum E 505, RVAp I, 78 no. 88; *LIMC* IV no. 1097). The native production is likely to continue through the Third Century BC and the more schematic specimens are possibly later, as indicated by a specimen in the votive deposit of Castelvecchio Subequo (van Wonterghem 1973, pl. 7 fig. 8) including a coin from the First Century BC.

Between 1994 and 1999 the Soprintenza Archeologica per l'Abruzzo carried out excavations at Fonte Sant'Ippolito at Corfinio, during which a small sanctuary was found. In a carefully arranged deposit near the temenos wall more than 150 statuettes, mainly representing Herakles/Hercules, were found. The deposit was presumably laid down in connection with the abandoning of the sanctuary, most likely caused by the events provoked by the Social War.

In the sanctuary were found eleven dedications, three in the Pelignian dialect, of which one specifically mentions *Hercle* as recipient.The other eight inscriptions are in Latin. The sanctuary seems to have been frequented from the early to the late Hellenistic period, with the greatest concentration from the Second Century BC. Cf Biella 2015, VIII-XV, figs. 1-2. Appendix II, 95 f. and *passim*.

Another bareheaded Herakles, but of a different style, is represented by Cat. 96 and 97. Parallels are found in the votive deposits of Caramanico and Carsòli, the latter covering the period about 320-220 BC according to coin evidence. These two statuettes fit into Colonna's group"Verona" which includes the majority of the Carsòli deposit (Colonna 1971, 175).

Cat. 100-103 are flattish and with a diagonal shoulderline, being very remote derivations of the Greek or Italiote prototype. There is a parallel in the above-mentioned deposit of Castelvecchio Subequo, to the later period of which these crude figurines most likely belong.

CAT. 92. HERAKLES BAREHEADED.
LION-SKIN OVER LEFT ARM

Inv. no. 13340.
H.: 11,9 cm.
Provenance: Unknown.
Acquisition: 1953. Bought from private collector, Copenhagen.
Bibliography: Unpublished.
Technique: Smooth surface. Dark brown patina. Missing: Right hand with weapon, left foot. Deep notch (faulty casting) under right knee.

Beardless Herakles brandishing weapon, now missing, in raised right hand. Left arm, with lion-skin, stretched forward, holding object (bow?). Standing on right leg, left bent and set to the side. Broad shoulders and neck, long torso, breastbone indicated by furrow, pectorals modelled. Flat skull, long face, short prominent nose, almond-shaped eyes, outer corner placed lower than inner. Small sharply defined mouth, small, prominent chin. Hair radiating from crown and nape of neck over forehead and ears.

Cf Colonna 1970, no. 493 pl. 121 (Chieti Mus.), group "Baranello"; nos. 525-526. pl. 129, Sulmona Mus.Civ. nos. 88, 108, group"Sulmona", Maestro C, very close, same hand. Biella 2015, I.a23, pl. 7 b-c, Santuario di Corfinio.

Cat. 92. Ca. 1:1.

Sabellian.
Prototype Fourth Century BC.
Third Century BC.

CAT. 93. HERAKLES BAREHEADED.
LION-SKIN OVER LEFT ARM

Inv. no. 3763.
H.: 9,3 cm.
Provenance: Unknown.
Acquisition: 1891. Bought in Rome from private collector.
Bibliography: Unpublished.
Technique: Greyish-green patina. Smooth surface.

Beardless Herakles brandishing now missing, weapon in raised right hand with cylindrical hole. Left arm, with lion-skin, lowered and stretched forward, thumb and index finger grasping now missing object. Standing on right leg, left bent and set forward. Broad neck and shoulders, long torso, pectoral and spine modelled. Rather flat skull, large face, prominent nose, small mouth with broad lips, small chin. Hair over forehead radiating from crown and in oblique furrows over nape of neck.

Cf Walters 1899 1274. Mon Ant X, c. 262, fig.11 b, Mus. Civ.Alfidena. Lebel 1961, pl. XL,1. *Italia Settentrionale* 1964, no. 316, pl. 80,163, votive deposit Gretta, Trieste (close). Colonna 1970, "group Sulmona" esp. pl. 129, nos. 525-526, Maestro C, very close, same hand (?).

Sabellian.
Prototype Fourth Century BC.
Third Century BC.

Cat. 93. Ca. 1:1.

CAT. 94. HERAKLES BAREHEADED. LION-SKIN OVER LEFT ARM

Inv. no. ABa 224.
H.: 11,8 cm.
Provenance: Unknown.
Acquisition: 1825. With the collection of the Archbishop of Taranto.
Bibliography: Unpublished.
Technique: Fairly smooth surface, corroded in parts. Olive-green patina with vivid green spots. Missing: weapon and right thumb, left arm from under shoulder.

Beardless Herakles brandishing now missing weapon in raised right hand. Left arm lowered. Standing on right leg, left leg bent and set forward. Pectorals, knee-caps, nipples and navel indicated. Long, broad neck, flat skull. Hair radiating from crown, oblique furrows over nape of neck. Facial features blurred.

Cf Walters 1899, 1274, from S. Maria di Capua; Chieti 7309, Coll.Zecca, close; Chieti, 3252, Coll. Pansa, fairly close; Colonna 1970, no. 493 (Chieti), close; 487, pl. 121 (Ravenna inv. 162) group "Baranello" Master B very close, same hand; no. 490, pl. 122 (New York, MMA inv. 969.426.).

Sabellian.
Third Century BC.

Cat. 94. Ca. 1:1.

CAT. 95. HERAKLES BAREHEADED. LION-SKIN OVER LEFT ARM

Inv. no. ABa 226.
H.: 9,4 cm.
Provenance: Unknown.
Acquisition: 1825 with the collection of the Archbishop of Taranto.
Bibliography: Unpublished.
Technique: Surface matt. Dark brown patina with some green areas. Missing: right hand with weapon and object in left hand.

Cat. 95. Ca. 1:1.

Beardless Herakles brandishing weapon, now missing, in raised right hand. Left arm, with lion-skin, stretched forward, hand clasping now missing object. Standing on right leg, left leg bent and set a little forward. Pectorals and knee-caps modelled. Rather flat skull, broad neck, long face, straight nose, outer corner of eyes placed lower than inner. Small mouth and small prominent chin. Hair radiating from crown and nape of neck.

Cf Italia Settentrionale, pl. LXXX,163, Trieste, Mus. Civ., stipe votiva. Colonna 1970 no. 489, pl. 121 "Group Baranello", Maestro B (close). van Wonterghem 1973, pl.VII, fig. 8, votive deposit, Castelvecchio Subequo (Paeligni).

Sabellian.
Prototype Fourth Century BC
Third Century BC.

Cat. 96. Ca. 1:1.

CAT. 96. HERAKLES BAREHEADED. LION-SKIN OVER LEFT ARM

Inv. no. 1250 g.
H.: 10,2 cm.
Provenance: unknown.
Acquisition: 1878/79. Given by Mrs. Bech, Valbygaard.
Bibliography: Unpublished.
Technique: Matt surface. Black patina. Missing: Right arm from under elbow. Left arm from under shoulder. Right foot.

Beardless Herakles brandishing now missing weapon in raised right hand. Left arm lowered. Standing on right leg, left advanced, touching ground with whole sole. Torso vaguely modelled. Head small, almond-shaped eyes, small aquiline nose. Back of head rather flat. Hair indicated by transversal grooves at back and vertical grooves coming forward over forehead.

Cf Fleischer, 1967, pl. 90,163 a. Anticka Bronza u Jugoslaviji 1844-1969, no. 107. Reinach, Rép.St. III, 69,3 (Rouen). Chieti 3287, flat back of head, same stance. Chieti 3189, Coll. Pansa (close). For original type, Cederna 1951, 186 fig. 6; 189 fig. 7,1, votive deposit, Carsòli). Colonna 1971, pl. 25, fig. 5 (Group"Verona").

Sabellian.
Third to Second Century BC.

**CAT. 97. HERAKLES BAREHEADED.
LION-SKIN OVER LEFT ARM**
Inv. no. 1250 h.
H.: 8,8 cm.
Provenance: unknown.
Acquisition: 1878/79. Given by Mrs. Bech, Valbygaard.
Bibliography: Unpublished.
Technique: Surface a little pitted. Dark brown patina. Right leg broken off over ankle, part of left foot missing.

Cat. 97. Ca. 1:1.

Beardless Herakles brandishing now missing weapon in raised right hand. Left arm, with lion-skin flying out horizontally, stretched out, hand with cylindrical perforation for now missing object. Resting on right leg, left leg bent and set forward. Long, vaguely modelled torso. Small round head. Features effaced. Low forehead. Hair radiating from crown of head.

Cf Cat. 96 (inv. 1250 g). Cederna 1951, 189, fig. 7,1, votive deposit, Carsòli. *Italia Settentrionale* 1964, pl. 80, 165 no. 315, Gretta votive deposit (Trieste). Colonna 1971, pl. 25, fig. 5 (Group"Verona"). Borell 1989, no. 59, pl. 27. (Heidelberg).

Sabellian.
Third Century BC.

CAT. 98. HERAKLES BAREHEADED. LION-SKIN OVER LEFT ARM

Inv. no. 1250 c.
H.: 6,8 cm.
Provenance: Unknown.
Acquisition: 1878/79. Given by Mrs. Bech, Valbygaard.
Bibliography: Unpublished.
Technique: Surface smooth. Dark brown patina. Missing: Right hand with club, left arm from shoulder, both legs from knees.

Cat. 98. Ca. 1:1.

Herakles brandishing club, now missing, in raised right hand. Left arm lowered. Standing on right leg, left a little advanced. Long, vaguely-modelled torso. Nipples indicated by dots. Head tilted toward left shoulder. Head small and round. Plastic eyeballs obliquely set, outer corner lower than inner. Hair radiating from top of crown in two rows of crescent-shaped curves.

Cf Colonna 1970, no. 624, 153 = Di Niro 1977, 30 no. 4, pl. 4, from Bonefro, now Chieti inv.781 (group"Cosenza", Master C). *Prima Italia* 1981, 205 no. 149, votive deposit, Gretta (Trieste, inv. 3477 = Guida/ Ruaro Loseri 1978 no. 12 = Gaheis, Archeografo Triestino, 4, 1908, 242, pl. I top left.

Prototype Fourth Century BC, but production, possibly in the Adriatic coastal area, indubitably continues into the Second or First Century BC.

CAT. 99. HERAKLES BAREHEADED. LION-SKIN OVER LEFT ARM

Without inv. no.
H.: 6,6 cm.
Provenance: Unknown.
Acquisition: Unknown.
Bibliography: Unpublished.
Technique: Surface fairly smooth. Greenish and black patina.

Beardless Herakles (?) brandishing club, now missing, in raised right hand, which has vertical cavity for object. Left arm lowered and stretched out, ending in shapeless lump. Standing frontally on both feet, legs apart. Large round head, broad temples, small chin. Low forehead, large almond-shaped eyes. Hair indicated by dots on scull. Nipples and navel indicated by almond-shaped impressions. Prominent sex.

Cf Cat. 98 (inv. 1.250c). *Padova Preromana* 1976, 192 no. 7, pl. 35,9 found in Padova outside Porta S. Giovanni in 1893 (very close). P.C. Guida 1989, nos. 8-11, from near Aquileia.

Northeast Italy.
Local derivation of Hellenistic type.

Cat. 99. Ca. 1:1.

CAT. 100. HERAKLES BRANDISHING CLUB. BAREHEADED. LION-SKIN OVER LEFT ARM

Inv. no. 13396.
H.: 6,1 cm.
Provenance: Unknown.
Acquisition: 1953. Bought from private collector.
Bibliography: Unpublished.
Technique: Surface smooth. Dark green to black patina. Right arm missing from over elbow.

Cat. 100. Ca. 1:1.

Beardless Herakles brandishing weapon in raised right hand. Left arm, with lion-skin, lowered and stretched forward. Standing on right leg, left leg bent and set forward. Torso vaguely modelled. Navel indicated. Head round and small. Nose pointed, mouth small and straight, large eyes indicated by punched circles. No forehead. Hair indicated by thick plastic rolls emanating from back of head.

Cf Italia Settentrionale, pl. LXXX, 164, Trieste, Mus.Civ. stipe votiva.

Anticka Bronza u Jugoslaviji 1844-1969, no. 108, from Celje (Celeia). Adam 1984 no. 284 (close). Chieti 7304, Coll. Zecca (close). Papi 1991, 142 no. 15, Chieti 852, from Caramanico (close). Biella 2015, I.a.12, pl. 5 a-b, Santuario di Corfinio.

Sabellian.
Third Century BC or later.

**CAT. 101. HERAKLES BAREHEADED.
LION-SKIN OVER LEFT ARM**

Inv. no. 1250 i.
H.: 6,7 cm.
Provenance: Unknown.
Acquisition: 1878/79. Given by Mrs. Bech, Valbygaard.
Bibliography: Unpublished.
Technique: Surface pitted. Dark brown to black patina.
Right arm missing from under shoulder.

Cat. 101. Ca. 1:1.

Beardless Herakles brandishing weapon in raised right hand. Left arm, with lion-skin, lowered and stretched forward. Standing on right leg, left leg bent and set to the side. Body leaning slightly backwards. Torso vaguely modelled. Nipples and navel indicated. Head round and small. Triangular nose. Large round eyes indicated by punched circles. No forehead. Hair arranged in small thick rolls radiating from back of head.

Cf Cat. 100 (inv. 13396); Cat. 102 (inv. 1250 e. van Wonterghem 1973, pl. VII, fig 8, Castelvecchio Subequo votive deposit including coin of First Century BC. Adam 1984 no. 284.

Second to First Century BC.

**CAT. 102. HERAKLES BAREHEADED.
LION-SKIN OVER LEFT ARM**

Inv. no. 1250 e.
H.: 6,4 cm.
Provenance: Unknown.
Acquisition: 1878/79. Given by Mrs. Bech, Valbygaard.
Bibliography: Unpublished.
Technique: Surface a little corroded. Green patina, rubbed off on left shoulder and under right arm.
Missing: Legs broken off at knees.

Cat. 102. Ca. 1:1.

Beardless Herakles brandishing (missing) weapon in raised right hand. Left arm, with lion-skin, lowered, hand closed. Torso long and somewhat contorted. Head round, eyes indicated by punched circles in the same way as the nipples. No forehead, hair radiating from low point at back of head.

Cf Cat. 100 (inv. 13396), Cat.101 (inv. 1250 i,). Chieti 3287. Adam 1984 no. 284.

Third Century BC.

Cat. 103. Ca. 1:1.

Cat. 104. Ca. 1:1.

CAT. 103. HERAKLES BAREHEADED. LION-SKIN OVER LEFT ARM

Inv. no. ABa 230.
H.: 8,6 cm.
Provenance: Unknown.
Acquisition: 1825. From the collection of the Archbishop of Taranto
Bibliography: Unpublished.
Technique: Black patina, matt surface. Missing: Right arm from elbow.

Beardless Herakles brandishing now missing weapon in raised right hand. Left arm, with lion-skin, stretched to the side. Standing on right leg, left leg advanced, heel free of ground. Long torso, vaguely modelled. Small, round head, flat at the back. Large round eyes, small, short nose, low forehead. Hair indicated by grooves forming a fringe and by transversal grooves at back.

Cf Colonna 1971, pl. 25 fig. 5, (Group"Verona"). Chieti 4361 from Carsòli, matt green-olive patina, same lion-skin, same stance, close. For stance, cf van Wonterghem 1973, pl.IX, fig. 11, Antiquarium of Corfinio, Third Century BC.

Sabellian.
Third Century BC.

CAT. 104. HERAKLES BRANDISHING CLUB. BAREHEADED. LION-SKIN OVER LEFT ARM

Inv. no. ABa 232.
H.: 7,8 cm.
Provenance: Unknown.
Acquisition: 1825. From the collection of the Archbishop of Taranto.
Bibliography: Unpublished.
Technique: Smooth surface. Brown patina. Missing: both feet.

Beardless Herakles brandishing weapon in raised tight hand. Left arm with lion-skin stretched forward. Standing on right leg, left leg advanced. Long modelled torso. Small, round head. Large eyes, small nose, smiling mouth, small chin. Hair radiating from crown. Large ears. Lion-skin has a herring-bone pattern.

Cf Chieti 3205, more striding, apple in left hand. Maiuri 1926, 249 fig. 2 left, from Sepino (very close).

The small votive deposit presumably antedates the destruction of Saepinum by the Romans in 293 BC.

Sabellian.
Fourth Century BC.

CAT. 105. HERAKLES BAREHEADED. LION-SKIN OVER LEFT ARM

Inv. no. ABa 45.
H.: 12,6 cm.
Provenance: Unknown.
Acquisition: 1813 in the Royal Danish Kunstkammer (bought on Etatsråd West's auction. Spengler 68).
Bibliography: Unpublished.
Technique: Surface fairly smooth. Dark brown patina.
Missing: Right lower arm and hand.

Beardless Herakles brandishing weapon, now missing, in raised right hand. Left arm, with lion-skin, lowered. The lion-skin is shaped like a fairly thin piece of material, forming a hollow at the back. Vertical rows of round impressions indicate the fur. In left hand an apple. Standing on left leg, right leg bent and set forward. Torso, front and back, finely modelled. Leg muscles and knee-caps also modelled. Skull short and round. Head tilted toward left shoulder. Wavy strands of hair radiating from top of crown. Small face with blurred features. Ears indicated, free of hair.

Cf Chieti, inv. 14106, from Villa Fonsina, fairly close, but more "local", legs "reversed", but same type. Chieti inv.10105, same prov., more "local", nipples indicated, deep spine furrow. Maiuri1926, 249, fig. 2 left, from Sepino (prov. di Campobasso). For style cf *Italia Settentrionale* 1964, pl. I,3 (votive deposit, Gretta, Trieste).

Sabellian.
Classical prototype and, like Cat. 104, presumably before 293 BC.

Cat. 105. Ca. 1:1.

CAT. 106 HERAKLES, YOUNG, BEARDLESS, HOLDING CLUB IN LEFT ARM. LION-SKIN HANGING FROM LEFT ARM. RIGHT ARM STRETCHED FORWARD HOLDING OBJECT

Inv. no. 823.
H.: 11,7 cm.
Provenance: Said to be from Magna Graecia.
Acquisition: 1874. Bought in Rome.
Bibliography: Unpublished.
Technique: Smooth surface. Missing object in hands. A few superficial scratches on right shoulder. Olive-green patina.

Cat. 106. Ca. 1:1.

Beardless Herakles brandishing weapon in raised right hand. Left arm advanced with lion-skin floating back, hand with cylindrical hole for now missing object. Bending both knees, right leg set to the side, heel free of ground. Figure leaning backwards. Head slightly tilted toward left shoulder. Torso front and back finely modelled with many details. Small buttocks. Knees and calves also modelled in detail. Fingers and toes indicated. Small, round face with rather vague features. Eyes round, set closely together, small nose and narrow, straight lips, small, round, slightly receding chin. Hair arranged in roll over forehead and neck. Tongue-shaped curls radiating from top of crown. On head a twisted diadem with five rosettes. On lion-skin plastic, very stylized head.

Cf de Ridder 1913 pl. 25,288. (more slender, upright). For stance: Popovic *et al.* 1969 no. 106 (from. Tujan Kod Bala). *LIMC* IV, Herakles no. 1093, Greek bronze statuette, 450-440 BC. de Ridder 1913, pl. 17,159 (Greek), *LIMC* IV, Herakles no. 1097, Apulian rf bell krater about 370 BC, showing statue of Herakles on top of column. LIMC IV Herakles no. 1087, Apulian rf pyxis, early Fourth Century BC. *LIMC* IV, Herakles no. 1081, Second-First Century BC.

Comment

The stance of Cat. 106 with both legs bent is unusual. Presumably it is derived from the Archaic striding type continuing into the Classical period with *eg* the Greek bronze statuette in Athens, Nat.Mus. inv. 14611 (*LIMC* IV Herakles no. 1093) and Louvre 159, de Ridder 1913, pl. 17, 159, the latter with the bow preserved in the left hand. The Apulian red-figure bell-krater British Museum E 505 by the Eton-Nika painter from about 370 BC, showing a statuette of Herakles on top of a column, seems to refer to a similar stance. The Apulian red-figure pyxis in Oldenburg (*LIMC* IV Herakles no. 1087) shows the more normal striding stance with the right leg stretched backwards, which also the Louvre 159 has. The rosettes on the twisted diadem of Cat. 106 point to a considerably later period, where examples of the Herakles Bibax type wear similar adornments, *eg* Adam 1984 no. 304, dated to the First Century BC, or the statuette in Vienna, von Sacken 1871, pl. 38,7, also from the First Century BC. A diadem with five rosettes is worn by a portrait of a Roman of the Tiberian period in the Ny Carlsberg Glyptotek (Johansen 1994 no. 81). The Herakles found at Tujan Kod Bala in former Yougoslavia is likely to be connected with the romanization of the area.

First Century BC to Second Century AD.

CAT 107. FRAGMENT OF HERAKLES STATUETTE

Inv. no. ABa 237.
L.: 5,2 cm.
Provenance: Unknown.
Acquisition: 1825. From the collection of the Archbishop of Taranto.
Bibliography: Unpublished.
Technique: Solid cast, separately, with socket for fastening. Dark brown patina with thin greenish layer. Surface matt.

Cat. 107. Ca. 1:1.

Fragment of Herakles statuette. Lion-skin with stylized plastic head hanging from left lower arm. Hand grasping now missing object.

Likely to be from type like Colonna 1970 no. 593, pl. 144 (Group"Avellino").

Sabellian.
Fourth to Third Century BC.

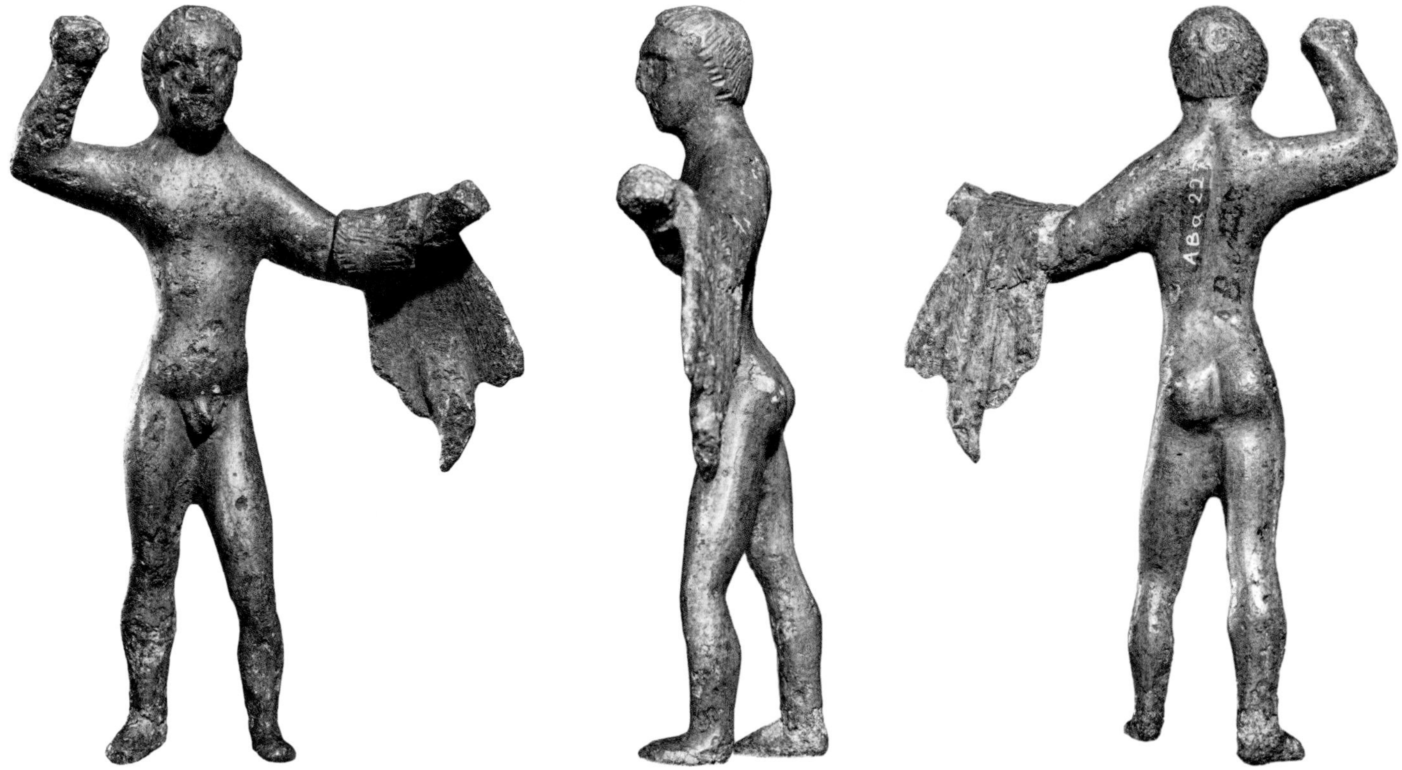

Cat. 108. Ca. 1:1.

CAT. 108. HERAKLES BAREHEADED.
LION-SKIN OVER LEFT ARM

Inv. no. ABa 227.
H.: 10 cm.
Provenance: Unknown.
Acquisition: 1825. From the collection of the Archbishop of Taranto.
Bibliography: Salskov Roberts 2002, 83 fig.1.
Technique: Olive-green patina. Surface smooth in parts, in parts corroded. Missing: objects in hands.

Beardless Herakles brandishing now missing weapon in raised right hand. Left arm, with lion-skin, lowered and stretched to the side. In left hand cylindrical perforation for object (bow?). Standing on right leg, left leg advanced. Long torso, pectorals, curved spinal furrow and abdomen modelled. Round head, short neck, facial features rather blurred due to corrosion. Two or three rows of short concentric strokes indicate hair. Also incisions on five slightly plastic folds indicate hair on lion-skin.

Cf Colonna 1970, pl. 111 no. 456. (Group"Bari"). Di Niro 1978, pl. 1, (Campobasso inv. 1006.) Adam 1984 no. 279. Papi 1992, 133 no. 20, 144 (Chieti 849), from Caramanico, (close).

Sabellian.
Prototype. Fourth Century BC. The parallel from Caramanico does, however, suggest a long life of the type, through the Second Century BC.

CAT. 109. HERAKLES BAREHEADED. LION-SKIN OVER LEFT ARM

Inv. no. 1250 d.
H.: 4,6 cm.
Provenance: Unknown.
Acquisition: In 1878/79. Given by Mrs. Bech, Valbygaard.
Bibliography: Unpublished.
Technique: Black patina with buff crust. Missing: Objects in hands, left leg from thigh; right leg from over knee.

Cat. 109. Ca. 1:1.

Beardless Herakles brandishing now missing weapon in raised right hand, left arm with lion-skin extended, hand having grasped an object. Resting on right leg. Torso modelled, deep cavity at waist at back. Large round head, large bulging eyeballs, small mouth. Hair arranged in roll around head. On crown wavy strands of hair.

Cf Cat. 108 (inv. ABa 227),

Sabellian.
Second Century BC.

CAT. 110. HERAKLES BAREHEADED. LION-SKIN OVER LEFT ARM

Inv. no. 1250 f.
H.: 7 cm.
Provenance: Unknown.
Acquisition: 1878/79. Given by Mrs. Bech, Valbygaard.
Bibliography: Unpublished.
Technique: Surface smooth. Dark green to black patina. Right foot broken off.

Cat. 110. Ca. 1:1.

Herakles, beardless, brandishing (missing) weapon in raised right hand, left arm lowered, with lion-skin. Standing on right leg, left leg bent and set forward. Muscles of torso vaguely modelled. Head round, large eyes. Tall crown of head, from which hairs radiate, indicated by deep herring-bone-like indentations.

Cf Colonna 1970, no. 552 pl. 136 ("Group Campobasso"). *Culture Adriatiche* 1978, pl. 166 from Caramanico. Adam 1984 no. 279.

Sabellian.
150-100 BC.

CAT. 111. HERAKLES BAREHEADED. LION-SKIN OVER LEFT ARM

Inv. no. ABa 228.
H.: 9,1 cm.
Provenance: Unknown.
Acquisition: 1825. From the collection of the Archbishop of Taranto.
Bibliography: Unpublished.
Technique: Black patina. Surface matt. Missing: left foot.

Beardless Herakles brandishing club in right hand. Indication of lion-skin over left elbow. Standing on right foot, left leg bent and advanced. Long, modelled torso. Small, round head, low forehead, large, obliquely set eyes, outer corner lower than inner. Short, broad and prominent nose. Straight mouth. Hair radiating from top of crown.

Cf Italia Settentrionale 1964, pl. 1,80-81, Trieste, Mus. Civ., stipe votiva di Gretta. Chieti 4568, from Sulmona, quite close. Di Niro 1977, 27 no. 1, from Larino (close). Papi 1991, nos. 13, 23 ,24, 25, all from Caramanico, Chieti Mus. Naz. inv. 850, 851, 844, 848, 853. Adam 1984 no. 285.

Sabellian.
End of Second-beginning of First Century BC.

Cat. 111. Ca. 1:1.

CAT. 112. NAKED MALE (HERAKLES?)

Inv. no. ABa 245.
H.: 6,6 cm.
Provenance: Unknown.
Acquisition: 1825. From the collection of the Archbishop of Taranto
Bibliography: Unpublished.
Technique: Surface partly corroded. Dark brown patina. Missing: Right arm broken off near elbow, left under shoulder, both legs at knee.

Beardless, naked male standing on right leg, left leg set slightly forward. The right arm stretched out, left arm lowered. Long, vaguely modelled torso. Round head, short hair. Features effaced. Nipples and navel indicated and shallowed out.

Cf Colonna 1970, pl. 150 no. 617, (Group"Cosenza"), mainly found along the Adriatic coast.

Sabellian.
Fourth-Third Century BC.

Cat. 112. Ca. 1:1.

CAT. 113. HERAKLES. BAREHEADED. LION-SKIN OVER LEFT ARM.

Inv. no. ABa 781.
H.: 8 cm.
Provenance: Unknown.
Acquisition: 1856/57. Bought in Rome.
Bibliography: Unpublished.
Technique: Surface matt. Blackish patina.

Beardless Herakles standing on right leg, the left leg slightly bent and set to the side. Right arm raised, cylindrical perforation in hand for now missing object. Left arm held a little back, broken off over the elbow. Hair arranged in soft locks around head with grooves radiating from crown. Tall forehead, irises hollowed out, short nose, open lips. Torso vaguely modelled. Spine indicated by groove. Back strongly S-shaped.

Cf Cat. 114 (inv. 1732). In many respects close to Cat. 114, the face of which is of a rather Etruscan style, whereas the facial features of this statuette seem later, perhaps well into the Roman period. Cf also Colonna 1970, pl. 140, no. 567 (Group"Bologna" Maestro A) and for stance, van Wonterghem 1973, pl. IX, fig.11, Antiquarium, Corfinio. (Third Century BC).

Cat. 113. Ca. 1:1.

Comment

The prototype of this statuette is indubitably from the end of the Fourth Century BC, but this specimen could be as late as the end of the Second or First Century BC.

Sabellian.
End of Second-First Century BC.

INTRODUCTORY NOTE TO CAT. 114-116 AND CAT. 121

Herakles standing, supporting himself with his right hand on the club and holding an object in the left hand, with the lion-skin draped over the left arm. The figure seems to refer to a statue placed in a public place, most likely in Herakleia, a city which issued a stater featuring such a Herakles holding a bow from about 350-200 BC (*LIMC* IV, 1-2, no. 281; Salskov Roberts 2002, 86).The well-known red-figured Apulian column-krater in New York from about 360-350 BC clearly depicts a statue with exactly these characteristics (*LIMC* IV, 1-2, no. 271). The facial features of Cat. 121 show a resemblance to the portraits of Ptolemy II Philadelphos (285-246 BC) and of his successor Ptolemy III Euergetes (246-221 BC) (Richter 1965, figs. 1781; 1792-1794; 1919-1819) and, accordingly, the small-scale production of this type should be placed in the Third Century BC.

On the Herakleia stater a jug is depicted in the field above the club, referring to representations of the hero pouring a libation at an altar, as specified on the Herakleia diobol (?) *SNG* Copenhagen I no. 1112. The altar is most likely that of Athena, whose close connection with Herakles the coins of Herakleia repeatedly stress.

Cat. 116 combines the types of Herakles supporting himself on the club with that of him holding the horn which he has wrenched off the forehead of Acheloos.

Cat. 114. Ca. 1:1.

CAT. 114. HERAKLES. HOLDING HORN OF ACHELOOS
Inv. no. 1732.
H.: 7,3 cm.
Provenance: Unknown.
Acquisition: 1882 bequested by V. Freund who had inherited it from his father, the sculptor H. Freund.
Bibliography: Salskov Roberts 2000, 63 fig. 1.
Technique: Surface smooth. Light brown to olive-green patina.

Beardless Herakles standing on right leg, the left leg bent and set backwards. Right arm advanced, hand holding oblong tapering object, likely to be interpreted as the horn of Acheloos. Short lion-skin draped over left arm, the rudimentary hand having held now missing object. Hair arranged in large roll around head, carved grooves radiating from crown. Large obliquely set eyes, bulging eyeballs, irises hollowed out. Short nose, dimple in upper lip, full and slightly open lips, corners turned downwards. Small, round chin. Torso modelled, groove indicating spine, back strongly S-shaped.

Cf for stance Cat. 113 (inv. no. ABa 781). Colonna 1970, no. 562 pl. 139 (Group"Bologna") = Adam no. 270. *Italia Settentrionale* 1964, pl.1,3, pl. LXXX, 162, (Gretta, stipe votiva. Trieste).

Prototype end of Fourth Century BC. Hairstyle derived from that of Alexander. Face of a rather Etruscan style, *cf* a certain affinity to some of the faces of the figures of the relief of the sarcophagus in the Ny Carlsberg Glyptothek HIN 61, Moltesen/Nielsen 1996 no. 28, esp. to the naked figure to the right of the seated Apollo. This is, in fact, consistent with the Etruscan tradition of Colonna's Group"Bologna".

Sabellian.
Second Century BC

Cat. 115. Ca. 1:1.

CAT. 115. HERAKLES. HOLDING HORN OF ACHELOOS
Inv. no. ABa 19.
H.: 6,2 cm.
Provenance: Unknown.
Acquisition: 1810. From the Høegh-Guldberg Collection.
Bibliography: Palagia 1988, *LIMC* IV Herakles, no.764 (as Herakles Bibax, ill).
Salskov Roberts 2000, 64, fig.3.
Technique: Surface corroded. Dark brown and green patina.
Missing: Parts of fillet or diadem. Lower legs and feet, end of club and top of object in right hand broken off.

Beardless Herakles standing on right leg, left leg set slightly back. Left arm, with lion-skin, holding club, right arm stretched forward. Right hand has held oblong, tapering object. Muscles of breast and torso vaguely modelled. Small nose, mouth slightly smiling. Hair arranged in wavy locks radiating from crown. Fillet, parts of which are missing.

Cf Cat. 114 (Inv. no. 1732). Caylus V, 1762, pl. 46,3-4. Guida/Ruaro Loseri 1978 no. 4 (Trieste inv. 2477 (Gretta votive deposit). Caravale 2003 no. 140.

For the motif, Morricone-Matini 1975 no. 55, 66-68, pls. XVIII-XXI, also ill. RA 1979, 1, 64 fig. 23.

For a study of the myth, Salskov Roberts 2000, 63 ff.

Comment

This version of Herakles is fairly rare in bronze. The horn has often been interpreted as a rhyton, but is more likely to refer to the victory of Herakles over Acheloos, whose horn he has torn off. A marble base in Istanbul from the First Century AD, Gozlan 1979, 62, fig. 21 shows a Herakles holding a horn in his left hand, while the defeated Acheloos is lying on the ground. A painting in the House of Yellow Wall in Ostia, from the Second Century AD has a Herakles holding a horn in his raised right hand and resting the club in his left arm in the company of a standing Acheloos, *ibid*. 63, fig. 22. Herakles adopts the same stance on the Anzio mosaic, *ibid*. 64, fig. 23.

The sculptural prototype may go back to the end of the Fourth Century BC, but there seems to have been a special interest in the motif in the Augustan period, continuing into the Second and Third Centuries AD, but mainly manifesting itself in mosaics and wall-painting.

First Century BC-Second Century AD.

Cat. 116. Ca. 1:1.

CAT 116 HERAKLES. HOLDING HORN OF ACHELOOS

Inv. no. 1255.
H.: 7,9 cm.
Provenance: Unknown.
Acquisition: 1878/79. Given by Mrs. Bech, Valbygaard.
Bibliography: Salskov Roberts 2000, 64, fig. 2.
Technique: Surface smooth. Dark olive-green patina. Casting fault on right foot. Part of original flat base cast with the feet preserved.

Beardless Herakles standing on right leg, left leg set a little back. The right arm is lowered, holding the club. The left arm, with the lion-skin hanging from it, is stretched forward, the hand holding a horn. The torso is modelled at the front, the abdomen pushed forward. The head turned a little to the left. The hair is arranged in a thick roll divided in the middle. Tall forehead, very large bulging eyeballs, irises hollowed out, directed upwards. Nose broad and flat, very full lips, small chin.

Cf Reinach III, 1904, 247,1 (bearded). *LIMC* IV, 1,744 ff. nos. 271 ff. Sculptural prototype dated to the early part of the Fourth Century BC as indicated by no. 271, red-figured Apulian column-krater, New York, MMA 50.11.4, from about 360-350 BC. *Cf* also coins from Herakleia, *SNG* Copenhagen I, nos. 1130-1131, diobols from 380-281 BC. For stance, marble relief in the Istanbul Museum, from Flavia Neapolis, Samaria, from the First Century AD, Gozlan 1979, 62 fig. 21.

The horn-shaped object in the left hand is most likely a horn, which refers to Herakles' struggle with Acheloos, from whom he wrenched one of his horns.

This Herakles type is fairly rare and belongs presumably to Roman Imperial times.

INTRODUCTORY NOTE TO CAT. 117-120

Herakles in a dynamic movement, adorned by a fillet with an ornament placed centrally over the forehead, is represented by Cat.117-120. There has been some discussion as to the nature of the ornament, ranging from a horn to a rudiment of the lion-skin. There can, however, not be much doubt that in the majority of cases it is the leaf-like ornament adorning victorious athletes, which is given to Herakles, underlining the victorious outcome of his efforts. Well-known examples of large statues of athletes honoured by a headband with a leaf-like ornament are the Marathon youth (Boardman *et al.* 1984, fig. 235) and the bronze statue from Fano on the Adriatic coast, for which a likeness to Seleukos I Nikator (312-280 BC) has been pointed out (Viacava 1994, figs. 7; 21). The latter figure may well have inspired the local production represented by Cat. 117, which is quite close – as far as stance is concerned – to the best Herakles in the Carsòli deposit (Cederna 1951, 189 fig. 7,1), which also indicated the Third Century BC for the more articulated specimens of this type.

The popularity of the victorious aspects of Herakles is evident in the Castelvecchio Subequo deposit, found about 20 km from Sulmona, famous for its temple dedicated to Herakles Victor. It contained about 28 Herakles statuettes of various types, small travertino bases, presumably for these statuettes, several fragments of larger Herakles statuettes, a large cippus of pyramidal section with two inscriptions in archaic Latin, mixed with Oscan elements and coins from the Second and First Centuries BC, the latest having been issued in 83 BC. The inscriptions of the cippus, which most likely served as a base for a fairly large cult figure, render two successive dedications to Herakles Victor by local donors. The chronological range of the types represented in this deposit should be the Second to the first half of the First Centuries BC (Bendinelli 1921, 284-290. van Wonterghem 1973, 36-48).

CAT. 117. HERAKLES. WEARING FILLET WITH CENTRAL ORNAMENT

Inv. no. ABa 225.
H.: 10,4 cm.
Provenance: Unknown.
Acquisition: 1825. With the collection of the Archbishop of Taranto.
Bibliography: Unpublished.
Technique: Surface corroded. Dark, greenish-grey patina.
Missing: Weapon, part of bow, both feet.

Beardless Herakles brandishing weapon in raised right hand. Left arm, with lion-skin, stretched forward. In left hand part of bow preserved. Both legs bent. Modelled torso. Spinal furrow indicated. Small round head, slightly inclined to the left. Hair arranged in roll over forehead and back. Over forehead, central ornament of fillet.

Cf Caylus V, 1762, pl. XLVI 46,1-2, from near Naples, Reinach. IV 1910, pl. 119,4. Cederna 1951, 189 fig. 7,1, from Carsoli. Adam 1984 no. 278, (close).

Sabellian.
Prototype second half of Fourth Century BC.
Second half of Third Century BC.

Cat. 117. Ca. 1:1.

CAT. 118. BEARDLESS HERAKLES BRANDISHING CLUB IN RAISED RIGHT ARM. CONICAL ORNAMENT OVER FOREHEAD

Inv. no. ABa 229.
H.: 10,1 cm.
Provenance: Unknown.
Acquisition: 1825. From the collection of the Archbishop of Taranto.
Bibliography: Unpublished.
Technique: Matt surface. Black patina. Missing: Left leg from knee, right leg from over ankle, possibly part of lion-skin, but fracture very smooth.

Beardless Herakles brandishing now missing weapon in raised right hand. Left arm with rudimentary lion-skin stretched to the side. Standing on right leg, left leg advanced. Long slim body, Pectorals vaguely modelled. Spinal furrow modelled. Round head, low forehead, almond-shaped eyes, outer corners lower than inner, very prominent nose, very full lower lip. Back of head flat. Hair radiating from crown. Over forehead conical excrescence (ornament on fillet?).

Cf Colonna 1970, pl. 150 no. 618 (Group "Cosenza"). Adam 1984 no. 278. Chieti 7307, Coll. Zecca, close.

Sabellian.
Third Century BC.

Cat. 118. Ca. 1:1.

CAT. 119. HERAKLES WITH EXCRESCENCE OVER FOREHEAD

Without inv. no.
H.: 7,7 cm.
Provenance: Unknown.
Acquisition: Unknown.
Bibliography: Unpublished.
Technique: Surface smooth. Dark green to black patina.
Missing: Right leg from knee, left arm from under shoulder, right hand and weapon.

Beardless Herakles brandishing weapon in raised right arm, weight on right leg, left leg advanced. Long torso vaguely modelled. Large Head without many details. Eyes indicated. Mouth straight. Short hair radiating from crown. Conical excrescence over forehead, ornament of fillet?

Cf Cat. 118 (inv. ABa 229). Adam 1984 nos. 278; 284. Papi 1991, 141 no. 9 (Chieti 847), from Caramanico. Chieti 4369, from Carsoli.

Sabellian.
Third Century BC.

Cat. 119. Ca. 1:1.

CAT. 120. HERAKLES. WEARING FILLET WITH CENTRAL ORNAMENT

Inv. no. 15173.
H.: 8,1 cm.
Provenance: Unknown.
Acquisition: 1976. Bought from the J. A. Bundgård Collection.
Bibliography: Unpublished.
Technique: Surface smooth. Black patina. Right arm broken off under elbow.

Cat. 120. Ca. 1:1.

Beardless Herakles brandishing now missing weapon in raised right hand. Lion-skin hanging over left arm, which is stretched forward, fist clenched. Standing on left leg, right leg set back. *Linea alba* and pectorals indicated. Punched circles for nipples. Small head with large eyes, a short, but big, nose, small chin. Hair radiating from point at crown rolled up over forehead and back. Fillet with central ornament.

Cf Papi 1991, 141 no. 9 (Chieti 847), from Caramanico, close.

Sabellian.
Third Century BC.

CAT. 121. HERAKLES RESTING HAND ON CLUB
Inv. no. ABa 234.
H.: 11,2 cm.
Provenance: Unknown.
Acquisition: 1825. From the collection of the Archbishop of Taranto.
Bibliography: Antik-Cabinettet 1851, 74, note 58. Salskov Roberts 2002, 86 f., figs. 6-7.
Technique: Fairly even surface. Green and brown patina.

Beardless Herakles standing on right leg, left leg a little advanced and set to the side. Resting right hand on club, left hand stretched forward, holding object. Head turned to the left. Details of torso summarily modelled. Head small and round. Thick neck. Small aquiline nose, strongly marked raised eyelids, full, smiling lips. Hair arranged in roll around head, ears placed underneath. On crown, irregular plastic locks. Fillet with central conical ornament. Features of lion-head vaguely indicated.

Cf for stance Walters 1899, nos. 1258, 1261 from Korfu. Reinach 1897 I, 474, pl. 802 D, no. 1964 D (Florence); *idem* 1904,III, 63,8. Sculptural prototype dated to the early part of the Fourth Century BC. A statue may have stood in South Italy, as attested by *eg* Apulian rf column-crater New York MMA 50,11,4, *LIMC* IV, 1,745 no. 271 (360-350 BC). Coin from Herakleia, 281-272 BC, SNG Copenhagen I nos. 1110-1111. Profile of head close to that of Ptolemy II Philadelphos and that of his succesor Ptolemy III Evergetes, *eg* Richter 1965, figs. 1781; 1792-1794; 1818-1819.

Type of this statuette from about 240 BC.
Second half of Third Century BC and later.

Cat. 121.

Cat. 121. Ca. 1:1.

COMMENTARY TO CAT. NOS. 122-123

Herakles holding the club upright, supported against the left arm, from which the lion-skin hangs, and with the right arm akimbo, is not a frequent representation of the hero. In this collection there are only two, one of which comes from the collection of the Archbishop of Taranto. The club held in this manner is seen on a Roman marble version of a victorious Herakles in the Vatican, the original of which is ascribed to the school of Lysippos (Moreno 1995, 61, Cat. 4.6.1). The right arm has, however, presumably been raised, pointing to the wreath adorning the head, as is the case of the image represented on Bactrian coins, *eg* minted by King Demetrius I (190-171 BC) and King Lysias (155-130 BC) (Moreno 1995, Cat. 4.10.2; Cat. 4.10.4). The arm placed akimbo may be a feature derived from another Lysippean Herakles type, *eg* the resting Herakles from Sulmona, which holds the right hand grasping an apple, not on, but behind the hip (Moreno 1995, Cat. 4.14.1).

The type combining these two features may not refer to a large-size prototype, but may be an experimental version created in the Second Century BC by a workshop producing small-scale bronzes, continuing the Lysippean tradition. This version, however, did not become popular with the public for small-scale votives in Magna Graecia at the time, but found more favour in Roman times, as the Vatican marble and a small bronze in Brussels suggest (*LIMC* IV no. 612).

CAT. 122. HERAKLES. RIGHT ARM AKIMBO. CLUB UPRIGHT IN LEFT ARM

Inv. no. ABa 44.
H.: without tang. 11 cm.
Provenance: Unknown.
Acquisition: Before 1813 in The Royal Danish Kunstkammer.
Bibliography: Unpublished.
Technique: Smooth surface. Dark green patina. A little pitted, especially on left shoulder. Missing: end of club.

Beardless Herakles standing on right leg, left leg set to the side, slightly advanced. Right arm akimbo, left arm with lion-skin stretched forward, holding club upright. Muscles of torso and legs richly modelled. Skull dome shaped, face small and round. Plastic eyeballs, full lower lip. Hair arranged in two rows of curls around forehead and nape of neck. On crown locks are indicated by irregular curved strokes. Fillet. On club embossed circles.

Cf Walters 1899 1253-54. de Ridder 1913, pl. 45, no. 650. Debrecen Deri Müzeum 1975, E IV.4. van Wonterghem 1973, pl.VII, fig.8, Castelvecchio Subequo votive deposit, including coin from beginning of First Century BC. Adam 1984 no. 301, close. *LIMC* IV (1988), 759 no. 603.

Roman version of Herakles.
First Century BC.

Cat. 122. Ca. 1:1.

Cat. 123. Ca. 1:1.

CAT. 123. HERAKLES. RIGHT ARM AKIMBO. CLUB UPRIGHT IN LEFT ARM

Inv. no. ABa 235.
H.: 6,8 cm.
Provenance: Unknown.
Acquisition: 1825. From the collection of the Archbishop of Taranto.
Bibliography: Antik-Cabinettet, 74, note 58.
Technique: Surface uneven, somewhat corroded. Dark green patina.

Herakles standing on left leg, the right leg set to the side. Right arm akimbo, left hand holding club, which rests against the shoulder. Large lion-skin hanging from left arm. Head tilted a little toward right shoulder. Hair arranged in roll with fillet around head, irregular grooves covering the skull. Very low forehead, obliquely set triangular eyes. No other details of face. Nipples and navel indicated by punched circles.

Cf Walters 1899 nos. 1254, 1287. Reinach III, (1904), 65,3; 247,4. de Ridder 1913 pl. 45, no. 649. Di Niro 1978 no. 4, pl. IV. Adam 1984 nos. 301 and 303. *Samnium* 1991, pl. 8d, d48d, from Casacalenda (inv. 34905)

Derived from Hellenistic prototype like the piece from Casacalenda.
Second-First Century BC.

Cat. 124. Ca. 1:1.

CAT. 124. HERAKLES. LEFT ARM AKIMBO

Inv. no. 1250 b.
H.: with tang: 8,9 cm.
H.: without tang: 7,9 cm.
Provenance: Unknown.
Acquisition: 1878/79. Given by Mrs. Bech, Valbygaard.
Bibliography: Unpublished.
Technique: Dark green patina. Surface corroded. Lower right arm and tip of cloak missing.

Naked Herakles standing on right leg, the left leg very slightly bent and set back. Left arm akimbo, right stretched forward. Over left shoulder and arm is draped a small cloak or rudimentary lion-skin. Round face with rather blurred features, round eyes. Hair with central parting, radiating from crown of head. Over forehead wreath with central rosette-like ornament. Through left foot original nail.

Cf male worshippers Cat. nos. 76-77 (inv. nos. 1251c; ABa 579).

The stance with arm akimbo is most likely a variation from Roman times, *Cf LIMC* IV no. 614, from Pompeii; also nos. 603; 612; in marble, *ibid*. nos. 667; 674 etc.

Roman.

CAT. 125. HERAKLES WITH MULTIPLE WRAPPING OF LION-SKIN AROUND LEFT ARM

Inv. no. ABa 243.
H.: 11,4 cm.
Provenance: Unknown.
Acquisition: 1825. From the collection of the Archbishop of Taranto.
Bibliography: Unpublished.
Technique: Black patina. Matt surface.Missing: Right arm from under shoulder, Left leg from over knee. Part of bow in left hand.

Herakles standing on right leg, left leg set to the side. Lion-skin wrapped several times around left shoulder and arm. In left hand part of bow. Hair rolled up at the back of the head. Strands of hair emanating from central line on crown. Around forehead wreath or diadem. Flat face with marked joining eyebrows, bulging eyes, small nose, very full lips.

Cf Colonna 1970 no. 600 (Vienna VI 57) For multiple wrapping of lion-skin, tetradrachm of Thasos, minted after 146 BC, *SNG* Denmark II, pl. 20, nos. 1038, 1039, 1049. For style of face, Guida/Ruaro Loseri 1978 no. 10, Trieste Mus. Civ. Inv. 2460, votive deposit of Gretta.

Sabellian.
About 100 BC.

Cat. 125. Ca. 1:1.

CAT. 126. CLUB OF HERAKLES
Inv. no. ABa 263.
L.: 7,5 cm.
Provenance: Unknown.
Acquisition: 1825. From the collection of the Archbishop of Taranto.
Bibliography: Unpublished.
Technique: Surface matt. Dark green patina.

Cat. 126. Ca. 1:1.

Tapering club

The club may come from statuette of "Resting Herakles" *eg* Chieti 4340 from Sulmona, sanctuary of Hercules Curinus, Third Century BC. Moreno 1995, no. 4,14,1, 104. Some clubs were, however, dedicated by themselves, as *pars pro toto, eg Samnium* 1991, pl. 7d, d44a-c, from the Campochiaro sanctuary frequented from the Fourth through the Second Century BC. Mattiocco/van Wonterghem 1989, 53 fig. 15a, Chieti Mus.Naz., votive club from Sulmona, sanctuary of Herakles Curinus.

Fourth-Second Century BC.

FRAGMENTS OF HERAKLES STATUETTES

CAT. 127. FRAGMENT OF HERAKLES STATUETTE

Without inv. no.
H.: 3,1 cm
Prov,: Unknown.
Acquisition: Unknown.
Bibliography: Unpublished.
Technique: Blackish-green patina, rubbed off in places.

Fragment of right hand holding a club.

Cat. 127. Ca. 1:1.

CAT. 128. FRAGMENT OF HERAKLES STATUETTE

Without inv. no.
H.: 5,1 cm.
Provenance: Unknown.
Acquisition: Unknown.
Bibliography: Unpublished.
Technique: Solid cast. Matt surface. Black patina.

Fragment of statuette of Herakles. Lower left arm with lion-skin, hand holding club downwards. Plastic tufts on mane. Head and paws modelled.

Cf Babelon/Blanchet 1895, 560, found at Reims. Adam 1984. nos. 304-305.

Judging from the size of the lion-head this fragment must have belonged to a fairly large statuette, perhaps like the above-mentioned pieces in the Bibliothèque Nationale, thought by Adam to have been produced by a workshop in Samnium in the First Century BC.

Samnian.
First Century BC

Cat. 128. Ca. 1:1.

ANATOMICAL VOTIVES

CAT. 129. ANATOMICAL VOTIVE. HAND

Inv. no. 3094.
L.: 8,0 cm.
Provenance: Unknown.
Acquisition: 1886. Bought in Florence.
Bibliography: Unpublished.
Technique: Olive-green patina with verdigris areas. Verdigris corrosion on end of rivets. Surface partly smooth.

Right hand and arm, with flat finish from elbow upwards. Two large rivets with heads on the inside of the arm. Possibly made as part of statuette. Thumb held wide apart from other fingers, which are slightly curving backwards. Individual fingers indicated.

Cf Arch. Mus. Florence inv. 463, 464 from votive deposit at Fonte Veneziana, Arezzo, Studi Maetzke I, 1984, 122 pl. IV e. *Padova Preromana* 1976, 217, no. 34, pl. 43, S. Pietro Montagnon, Scapin votive deposit, Sixth-Third Century BC.

North Etruscan.
Sixth-Fifth Century BC or later.

Cat. 129. Ca. 1:1.

CAT. 130. ANATOMICAL VOTIVE. LEG
Inv. no. 3095.
H. with tang: 8,7 cm.
H. without tang: 7,3 cm.
Provenance: Unknown.
Acquisition: 1886. Bought in Florence.
Bibliography: Unpublished.
Technique: Solid cast with broad tapering tang. Olive-green patina, smooth surface chipped at extremities, where verdigris layer appears.

Cat. 130. Ca. 1:1.

Left leg, thigh tapering at top into finished edge. Calf and ankles indicated.

Cf Arch.Mus. Florence inv. 467, from votive deposit at Fonte Veneziana, Arezzo. Studi Maetzke I, 1984, 122, pl. IV,f. Santuari d'Etruria 1985, 174 ff.,177 f., 10,2-19. Comella 1982, pl. 95a inv. 4790 (same measurements: 8,7 cm). The votive deposit at Ara della Regina most likely belonged to a sanctuary nearby. Most of the votives are terracottas, only one leg, one nose, one ear and two fingers are in bronze. One terracotta leg has an Etruscan dedication mentioning the donor, but not the deity, who was, however, obviously concerned with health problems. Coins show the sanctuary to have been active from about 250 to 100 BC. *Padova Preromana* 1976,217 no. 32, pl. 43, S. Pietro Montagnon, Scapin votive deposit, sanctuary mainly frequented from Sixth to Third Century BC. Scarpignato 1986, 224, pl. IV, 8-9, from Bettona (Umbria). Fortuna/Giovannoni 1989, no. 63, from votive deposit at Falterona, Sixth-Fifth Century BC.

Cat. 130, inv. no. 3.095 is very close to the Archaic votives from Fonte Veneziana and Falterona, but the type seems to continue without much change.

North Etruscan.
Sixth-Fifth Century or later.

FRAGMENTS OF STATUETTES

CAT. 131. PAIR OF LEGS

Without inv. no.
H. without tang: 3,5 cm. With tang: 4,7 cm. (modern).
Provenance: Unknown.
Acquisition: Unknown.
Bibliography: Unpublished.
Technique: Lost wax casting, hollow, but filled with modern metal. Dark-green and brown patina.

Cat. 131. Ca. 1:1.

Fragment of statuette. Feet and legs from under knee. Weight on right leg.

Cf Sannibale 1995, 17 f.

Hellenistic.

CAT. 132. LEFT FOOT

Without inv. no
L.: 4,9 cm.
Provenance: Unknown.
Acquisition: Unknown.
Bibliography: Unpublished.
Technique: Solid cast. Surface fairly even, but matt. Dark green patina, verdigris and blue in fracture. Trace of large tang.

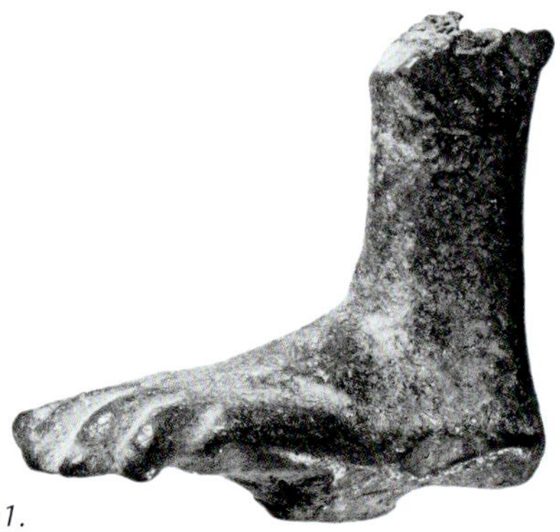

Cat. 132. Ca. 1:1.

Fragment of statuette. Left foot and lower leg. Second toe longer than big toe. Little toe rudimentary. Three middle toes bent, holding ground.

Hellenistic.

CAT. 133. LEFT FOOT

Without inv. no.
L.: 5,6 cm.
Provenance: Unknown.
Acquisition: Unknown.
Bibliography: Unpublished.
Technique: Solid cast. Under foot large lump from casting. Spotted dark-green patina. Matt surface.

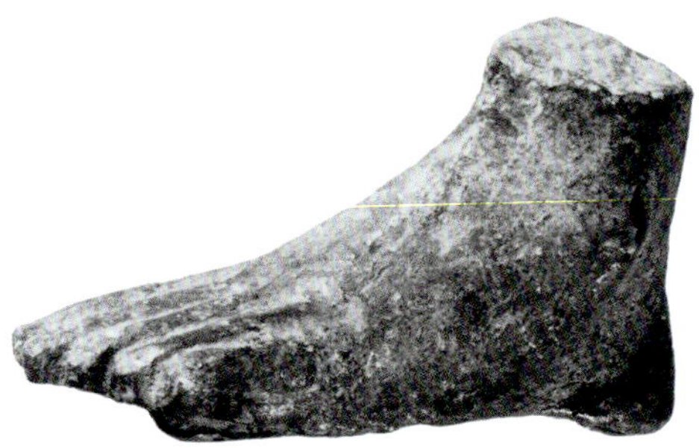

Cat. 133. Ca. 1:1.

Fragment of statuette. Left foot. Big toe shorter than second toe. Toes straight. Ankles (malleoli) indicated.

Hellenistic.

ANIMALS

CAT. 134. HORSE

Cat. 134. Ca. 1:1.

Inv. no. 5361.
L.: 8,4 cm with tail.
H.: 6,3 cm.
Provenance: Perugia.
Acquisition: 1903. Bought in Florence.
Bibliography: Unpublished.
Technique: Solid cast. Smooth surface. Greyish-green patina. Round hole, for original mounting? Under left hind hoof. The right front hoof, of which half is missing, has had a vertical hole.

Horse standing on four legs. Eyes, nostrils and muzzle indicated. Short mane indicated by obliquely set notches, strands of hair of tail by vertical furrows. Deep indentation on chest to indicate fold.

Cf Padova Preromana 1976, 176 f., pl. 30, 7; 10, votive deposit S. Daniele, "Second half of Fifth Century - first half of Fourth Century BC, North Umbrian or local workshop."; 201, 211 ff., pls. 41-42, several pieces from the votive deposit S. Pietro Montagnon, same period.

Cristofani 1985, 148 no. 38, Venice Arch.Mus. (Coll. Correr) 500-480 BC., Volterran workshop.

North Etruscan.
Fifth-Fourth Century BC

CAT. 135. TWO-HEADED DOG (CERBERUS?)

Inv. no. 2289.
H.: 7,1 cm.
L.: 9,4 cm.
Provenance: Unknown.
Acquisition: Bought in June 1885 in the Gréau Sale, Paris.
Bibliography: Coll. Gréau, Catalogue des bronzes antiques, (1-9-6, 1885), no. 890. Fossing, *NMArb* 1938, 45 fig. 2
Technique: Solid cast. Lower left front leg broken off. On left side of the larger head a damaged area, where most likely a third head was placed, are two small circular holes, possibly for fixing. Olive-green patina. Smooth surface except where chipped.

Cat. 135. Ca. 1:1.

Dog with two, possibly originally three heads. One head larger than the other preserved one. Long snout, open mouth with tongue sticking out. Eyes indicated by triangular indentations. Standing on three legs, the left front leg being lifted. Tail raised. Sex indicated. Body modelled.

Cf Babelon/Blanchet 1895 no. 793 (close). There are only a few examples of free-standing bronzes of Cerberus, but the figurine in Cabinet des Médailles, Paris, has the same dimensions and patina.

Cf for Cerberus in Etruria von Essen 1927, esp.p.6. The Cerberus Vanth Group Painter shows the three-headed dog sitting down, with a chain twined around the haunch. The hindmost head looking back toward the person pulling at its chain, Bandinelli/Giuliano 1973, 279 fig. 319.

Cerberus with one paw lifted follows the scheme of the Apulian volute-krater ascribed to the circle of the Lycurgos Painter (350-325 BC), *LIMC* VI, Kerberos no. 31.

The painting in the Tomba dei Rilievi of the Third Century BC has a crouching Cerberus with one head looking back, one paw raised and lifted snaketail.

Cerberus features as a coin design of Elea (Epirus) in the Fourth Century BC, of Capua, (Campania) in the Third Century BC and of an Etruscan mint (Vetulonia?), in the Fourth or Third centuries BC.

Fourth-Third Century BC.

Bibliography

Bibliography

Accademia etrusca 1985,
L'Accademia etrusca. Exhibition Catalogue, Cortona, Palazzo Casali 19 maggio-20 ottobre 1985. (edd. P. Barocchi/D.Gallo). Milan 1985.

Adam 1984
A. M. Adam, *Bronzes étrusques et italiques,*
Paris 1984.

Ammirati 1979-80
A. Ammirati, Bronzetti votivi etruschi e italici nelle Civiche Gallerie di Arte Antica, *"Musei Ferraresi", Bollettino Annuale* IX-X,1979-1980 (1982). Ferrara 1979-80.

Amorelli 1982
M. T. Amorelli, *I materiali archeologici preromani del Museo Oliveriano di Pesaro.*
Rome 1982.

Anati 1984
(ed. E. Anati), *I Sardi, La Sardegna dal Paleolitico all'età romana.*
Milan 1984.

Andrén 1967
A. Andrén, Il santuario della necropoli di Cannicella ad Orvieto.
StEtr XXXV, 1967, 41-85.

Antidoron 1983 = Antidoron, Festschrift Jürgen Thimme
Karlsruhe 1983.

Anticka Bronza u Jugoslaviji 1844-1969
Lj. B. Popovic et al.
(ed. Narodni Musei Beograd),
Belgrade 1969.

Antik-Cabinettet 1851, see
N. Breitenstein

AnnMuseoFaina = Annali per la Fondazione Claudio Faina, Orvieto.

Arezzo = Arezzo nell'antichità
G. Camporeale/G. Firpo (edd.)
Rome 2009.

Art and Technology.
A Symposium on Classical Bronzes, (edd. S. Doeringer/D.G. Mitten/A. Steinberg),
Cambridge Massachusetts/London 1970.

Bayet 1926
J. Bayet, *Herclé, Étude critique des principeaux monuments relatifs à l'Hercule étrusque.*
Paris 1926.

Babelon/Blanchet 1895
E. Babelon - J.-A. Blanchet,
Catalogue des bronzes antiques de la Bibliothèque Nationale.
Paris 1895.

Balty 1961a
J. Ch. Balty, Note sur un type italique de l'Hercule promachos,
Bull des Musées Royaux d'Art et d'Historie, sér. IV, XXXIII,
1961.

Balty 1961b
J. Ch. Balty, Un centre de production de bronzes figurés de l'Etrurie septentrionale, Volterra,
Bull de l'Inst Hist. Belge de Rome 33, 1961, 196.

Balty 1962
J. Ch. Balty, Dégradations successives d'un type d'Hercule italique, in *Hommage à Albert Grenier* (Collection Latomus LVIII), Brussels 1962, 197-215.

Bandinelli - Guiliano 1973
R. Bianchi Bandinelli - A. Giuliano, *Etruschi ed Italici prima del dominio di Roma.*
Milan 1973.

Banti 1965
L. Banti, *Die Welt der Etrusker.*
Stuttgart 1965.

Beazley Gifts 1967
Sir John and Lady Beazley Gifts 1912 /1966
Ashmolean Museum, Department of Antiquities, April 24 to June 2. June 27 to September 9.
London 1967.

Beazley/Magi 1941
J. D. Beazley/F. Magi, *La raccolta Benedetto Guglielmi nel Museo Gregoriano Etrusco* II,
Città del Vaticano 1941.

Bendinelli 1920
G. Bendinelli,
Bronzi votivi italici del Museo Nazionale di Villa Giulia,
MonAnt XXVI, 1920.

Bendinelli 1921
G. Bendinelli, Superaequum. Castelvecchio Subequo (Aquila).
NS 1921, 284-290.

Bentz 1992
M. Bentz, *Etruskische Votivbronzen des Hellenismus.*
(Biblioteca di"Studi Etruschi" No. 25).
Firenze 1992.

Bérard-Azzouz 1997, *Les bronzes antiques du Musée de l'Éphèbe.*
Collections sous-marines.
Musée de l'Éphèbe,
Agde 1997.

Bianchi Bandinelli/Giuliano 1973
R. Bianchi Bandinelli/A. Giuliano, *Etruschi ed Italici prima del dominio di Roma.*
Milan 1973.

Bieber 1915
M. Bieber, *Die antiken Skulpturen und Bronzen des königliches Museum Friedericianum in Cassel.*
Marburg 1915.

Bieber 1961
M. Bieber, *The Sculpture of the Hellenistic Age.*
New York 1961.

Biella 2015
M. C. Biella, *I bronzi votivi dal santuario di Corfinio, Localitá Fonte Sant'Ippolito.*
(Biblioteca di "Studi Etruschi"54).
Rome 2015.

von Bissing 1928
Fr. W. von Bissing, Die sardinischen Bronzen, *RM* 43, 1928, 19-89.

Boardman et al. 1984
J. Boardman/J. Dörig/W. Fuchs/M. Hirmer, *Die griechische Kunst.*
Munich 1984.

Boardman 1988
J. Boardman, s.v. Herakles,
LIMC IV, 1988, 728-738; 796-827; 832-838.

Boardman 1990
J. Boardman, *s.v.* Herakles,
LIMC V, 1990, 1-16; 67-73; 111-133; 141-160; 166-172; 176-192.

Bocci Pacini 1984
P. Bocci Pacini, Alcuni bronzetti arcaici dalla "Fonte Veneziana" di Arezzo, in
Studi di antichità in onore di G. Maetzke,
Rome 1984, 119-123.

Boethius et al. 1962
A. Boetius et al., *Etruscan Culture. Land and People.*
Malmoe/New York 1962.

Borell 1989
B. Borell, *Statuetten, Gefässe und andere Gegenstände aus Metall.*
Mainz a/R 1989.

von Bothmer 1951
D. von Bothmer, Enkaustes Agalmaton,
BMetrMus 1951, 156-161.

Boucher 1970
S. Boucher, *Bronzes grecs, hellénistiques et etrusques des Musées de Lyon.*
(Travaux édités sous les auspices de la ville de Lyon II)
Lyon/Paris 1970.

Breitenstein 1941
N. Breitenstein, *Catalogue of Terracottas, Cypriote, Greek, Etrusco-Italian and Roman.*
Copenhagen 1941.

Breitenstein 1951
N. Breitenstein,"Christian VIII's Vasecabinet", in
Antik-Cabinettet 1851 udgivet i Hundredaaret af Nationalmuseet,
Copenhagen 1951, 62-76.

Briguet 1959
M.-F. Briguet, Deux groupes de figurines étrusques archaïques,
La Revue des Arts 9, 3, 1959, 132-135.

Brizio 1890
E. Brizio, Statuette di bronzo e sculture marmoree scoperte presso la Villa Ruffi,
NS 1890, 208-209.

Bulle 1930
H. Bulle, Zwei griechische Bronzen. II. Krieger von Aphiona,
AM LV, 1930, 181-190.

Buranelli 1989
F. Buranelli, *La Raccolta Giacinto Guglielmi 23 maggio - 29 luglio 1989, Exhibition Catalogue.*
Rome 1989.

Camporeale 1969
G. Camporeale, Osservazioni su due piccoli busti bronzei da Chiusi.
ArCl 2, 1969, 39-52.

Camporeale 2009
G. Camporeale, Arezzo in età etrusca: Profilo storico, in *Arezzo*, 55-82.

Carabatea 1997
M. Carabatea,
Herakles and a"Man in Need?" in
Greek Offerings, Essays in honour of John Boardman.
Oxford 1997, 131-143.

Caravale 2003
A. Caravale, *Museo Claudio Faina di Orvieto.*
Bronzetti votivi (Catalogo dei beni culturali dell'Umbria).
Perugia 2003

Carratelli 1996
G. Pugliese Carratelli, *The Western Greeks. Classical Civilization in the Western Mediterranean.*
London 1996.

Caylus 1761
Comte de Caylus, *Recueil d'Antiquités Egyptiennes, Etrusques, Grecques et Romaines.*

Paris	I	1761
	II	1756
	III	1759 (et Gauloises)
	IV	1761
	V	1762
	VI	1764
	VII	1767

Cederna 1951
A. Cederna,
Carsòli. Scoperta di un deposito votivo del II secolo av.Cr.
NS 1951, 169-224.

Cianfarani 1978
V. Cianfarani, *Culture adratiche antiche d'Abruzzo e di Molise.* I-II.
Rome 1978.

Coles/Harding 1979
J. Coles and A. Harding, *The Bronze Age in Europe.*
London 1979.

Colonna 1961
G. Colonna, *s.v.Italica, Arte,* in
EAA IV, 251-274, esp. 268 ff.

Colonna 1970
G. Colonna, *Bronzi votivi Umbro-Sabellici a figura umana.*
Florence 1970.

Colonna 1971
G. Colonna, Problemi dell'arte figurativa di età ellenistica nell'Italia Adriatica, in
Atti del I Convegno di Studi sulle antichità adriatiche, 172-177.
Chieti-Francavilla 1971.

Colonna 1976-77
G. Colonna, La dea etrusca Cel e i santuari del Trasimeno,
Rivista storica dell'Antichità 6-7, 1976-77, 44-62.

Comella 1982
A. Comella, *Il deposito presso Ara della Regina.*
Rome 1982.

Comstock/Vermeule 1971
M. Comstock and C.Vermeule, *Greek, Etruscan and Roman Bronzes in the Museum of Fine Arts, Boston.*
Boston 1971.

Cristofani 1979a
M. Cristofani, La Testa Lorenzini e la scultura tardo arcaica in Etruria settentrionale,
StEtr 47, 1979, 85-92.

Cristofani 1985
M. Cristofani, *I Bronzi degli Etruschi.*
Novara 1985.

Culture adriatiche antiche d'Abruzzo e di Molise. I-II. See Cianfarani 1978.

Danish National Museum Guide 1968
Greece, Italy and the Roman Empire (P. Mortensen/H. Salskov Roberts edd).
Copenhagen 1968.

Danish Mational Museum Guide 1994
(J. Lund/B. Bundgaard Rasmussen edd).
Antiksamlingen. Grækere, etruskere, romere.
Copenhagen 1994.

De Agostino 1961
A. De Agostino, Populonia (Livorno). Scoperte archeologiche nella necropoli negli anni 1957-1960,
NS 1961, 63-102.

De Agostino 1971
A. De Agostino, *La necropoli arcaica di Populonia.*
Rome 1971.

Debrecen Deri Müzeum 1975
(ed. J. G. Szilágyi) *Exhibition Catalogue 1975.*
(Bulletin du Musée Roi Saint-Etienne, Sér. D. No. 102)

Degrassi 1981
N. Degrassi, *Lo Zeus stilita di Ugento.*
Rome 1981.

Del Chiaro 1974
M. A. Del Chiaro, A Newly Discovered Etruscan Town.
Archaeology 27, no. 4, 1974, 270-273.

Del Chiaro 1975
M. A. Del Chiaro, The Archaic Bronze Kouros from Ghiaccio Forte,
AJA 79, 1975, 84 f.

Del Chiaro 1976
M. A. Del Chiaro, Four archaic Etruscan Bronze statuettes in Santa Barbara, California.
AJA 80, 1976, 301-302. Pls. 56-57.

Dietz 1981
S. Dietz, Votivbronzer fra Sardiniens forhistorie, in *Studies P. V. Glob*, 1981, 222-236.
Copenhagen 1981.

Di Niro 1977
A. Di Niro 1977, Il culto di Ercole. Fra i Sanniti Pentri e Frentani. Nuove Testimonianze, in
Documenti di Antichità Italiche e Romane IX, 1977.

Di Niro 1978
A. Di Niro, *Piccoli bronzi figurati nel Museo di Campobasso.*
Salerno 1978.

Di Niro 1984
A. Di Niro, *Atti del XIII convegno di studi Etruschi e Italici, Manfredonia 21-27 giugno 1980,*
Florence 1984, 35-43.

Di Stefano 1975
C. A. Di Stefano, *Bronzetti figurati del Museo Nazionale di Palermo.*
Rome 1975.

von Essen 1927
C. C. von Essen, *Did orphic Influence in Etruscan Tomb Painting exist? Studies in Etruscan Tomb Paintings I.*
Amsterdam 1927.

Emilia e Romagna 1985
La Romagna tra VI e IV sec.a.C. nel quadro della protostoria dell'Italia Centrale,
Atti del Convegno, Bologna, 23-24 ottobre 1982.
Imola 1985.

Etruria Padana 1960,
La Mostra dell'Etruria Padana e della città di Spina 12 settembre-31 ottobre 1960.
Bologna, Palazzo dell'Archiginnasio.
Bologna 1960.

Euphronios. 1990.
Atti del Seminario Internazionale di Studi, Arezzo 27-28 Maggio 1990
(edd. M. Cygielman et al.)
Milan 1991.

EVB
Richardson 1983
E. Richardson, *Etruscan Votive Bronzes. Geometric, Orientalizing, Archaic, I-II,*
Mainz a/R 1983.

Fedeli 1993
F. Fedeli et al., *Populonia e il suo territorio. Profilo storico-archeologico.*
Florence 1993.

Fleischer 1967
R. Fleischer, *Die römischen Bronzen aus Österreich.*
Mainz a/R 1967.

Fogolari 1950-51
G. Fogolari, Bronzetti etruschi e italici nel Museo del Teatro Romano di Verona.
StEtr 21, 1950-51, 343-374.

Fogolari 1952-53
G. Fogolari, Per un corpus dei bronzetti etruschi. Bronzetti etruschi e italici nel Museo del Teatro Romano di Verona,
StEtr 22, 1952-53, 286-304.

Formazione della città in Emilia Romagna 1987,
Exhibition Bologna, Museo Civico Archeologico, 26 settembre - 24 gennaio 1988.
Bologna 1987.

Formigli 1984
E. Formigli, *Nota technica,* in Bocci Pacini 1984, (*Studi Maetzke* 1984).
Rome 1984, 123.

Fortuna/Giovannoni 1989
A. M. Fortuna/F. Giovannoni, *Il Lago degli Idoli. Testimonianze etrusche in Falterona.*
Florence 1989.

Fossing 1938
P. Fossing, Kerberos.
NArb 1938, 43-48.

Franzoni 1980
L. Franzoni, *Bronzetti etruschi e itailici del Museo archeologico di Verona.*
Rome 1980.

Fuhrmann 1941
H. Fuhrmann, Archaeologische Grabungen und Funde. Regio IV. Sabina und Samnium. Caramanico.
AA 1941, 630f.

Furtwängler 1895
A. Furtwängler, *Masterpieces of Greek Sculpture.*
Reprint Chicago 1964.

Furtwängler 1903
A. Furtwängler, *Ein Hundert Tafeln nach den Bildwerken der Kgl. Glyptothek zu München.*
Munich 1903.

Furtwängler 1910
A. Furtwängler, *Beschreibung der Glyptothek.*
Munich 1910.

Gàbrici 1906
E. Gàbrici, Bolsena, Scavi nel sacellum della Dea Nortia sul Pozzarello, *MonAnt* XVI, 1906, 169-240.

Gaheis 1908
A. Gaheis, *Argheografo Triestino, Trieste, serie III, vol. IV, 1908.*
Trieste 1908, 239-47.

Galli 1918
E. Galli, Impruneta. Vestigia di un antichissimo santuario etrusco presso l'Impruneta.
NS 1918, 210-215.

Gardiner 1907
E. Norman Gardiner, Throwing the diskos.
JHS 27, 1907, 1-36.

Gardiner 1930
E. Norman Gardiner,
Athletics of the Ancient World.
Oxford 1930.

Gens Antiquissima Italiae 1991
Antichità dall'Umbria a New York.
Exhibition Catalogue, Grey Art Gallery, 9 settembre-2 novembre 1991,
Perugia 1991.

Gentili 1985
M. D. Gentili, *Statuette femminili.*
Arezzo 1985.

Ghirandini 1888
G. Ghirandini, Este. Intorno alle antichità scoperte nel fondo Baratela.
NS 1888, 71-127.

Giglioli 1935
G. Q. Giglioli, *L'Arte Etrusca.*
Milan 1935.

Giglioli 1954
G. Q. Giglioli, Bronzetti del territorio di Rimini.
StEtr XXIII, 1954, 13-24.

Glob 1981
Studies presented to P. V. Glob, Det skabende menneske, II.
Copenhagen 1981.

Gori 1737
A. F. Gori, *Museum Etruscum exhibens insignia veterum Etruscorum monumenta.* I-II.
Florence 1737.

Gori 1750
A. F. Gori, *Museum Cortonense in quo vetera monumenta comprehenduntur in Academia Etrusca.*
Rome 1750.

Gozlan 1979
S. Gozlan, Au dossier des mosaîques Héracléennes: Acholla (Tunisie), Cártama (Espagne), Saint-Paul-Lès-Romans (Gaule), *RA*, 1979, 35-92.

Gréau 1885
Collection Gréau. Catalogue des bronzes Antiques. 1-9 Juin 1885.
Paris 1885.

Greek Offerings.
Essays on Greek Art in honour of John Boardman.
(ed. O. Palagia).
Oxford 1997.

Gualandi 1970
G. Gualandi, Il santuario fontanile a Nord della città. (Marzabotto).
StEtr. 38, 1970, 217-223.

Gualandi 1974
G. Gualandi, Santuari e stipi votive dell'Etruria padana.
StEtr 42, 1974, 37-68.

Guida/Loseri 1965
P. Càssola Guida/L. Ruaro Loseri,
Arte e civiltà romana nell'Italia settentrionale dalla repubblica alla tetrarchia.
Catalogo della Mostra. Bologna 1964.
Bologna 1965.

Guida/Loseri 1978
P. Càssola Guida/L. Ruaro Loseri,
Bronzetti a figura umana dalle collezioni dei Civici Musei di Storia ed Arte di Trieste.
Venice 1978.

Guida 1989
P. Càssola Guida, *I bronzetti Friulani a figura umana tra protostoria ed età della romanizzazione.*
Rome 1989.

Guido 1963
M. Guido, *Sardinia.*
London 1963.

Haynes 1960
S. Haynes, The Bronze Priests and Priestesses from Nemi.
RM 67, 1960, 34-47.

Haynes 1971
S. Haynes, *Etruscan Sculpture.*
London 1971.

Haynes 1985
Sybille Haynes, *Etruscan Bronzes.*
London 1985.

Hellenismus in Mittelitalien,
Kolloquium Göttingen 5.-9. Juni, 1974, I.
Göttingen 1976.

Higgins 1954
R. A. Higgins, *Catalogue of the Terracottas in the Department of Greek and Roman Antiquities. British Museum.*
London 1954.

Hostetter 1986
E. Hostetter, *Bronzes from Spina* I. *The figural Classes.*
Mainz a/R 1986.

Höckmann 1982
U. Höckmann, *Staatliche Antikensammlingen München; Katalog der Bronzen* I, *Die Bronzen aus dem Fürstengrab von Castel San Mariano bei Perugia.*
Munich 1982.

Höckmann 2002
U. Höckmann, Der Duft der Blüten. Bronzestatuette eines Mädchens aus Volterra in München, in
Volterra (edd. S. Steingräber/H. Blanck, Mainz 2002, 53-58, figs. 72a-72d.

Hus 1975
A. Hus, *Les bronzes étrusques.*
(Collection Latomus vol. 139)
Brussels 1975.

Italia Settentrionale.
P. Càssola Guida/L. Ruaro Loseri, *Arte e civiltà romana nell'Italia settentrionale dalla repubblica alla tetrarchia.*
Catalogo della Mostra, Bologna 1964.
Bologna 1965.

Jantzen 1937
U. Jantzen, Bronzewerkstätten in Grossgriechenland und Sizilien, *Jahrbuch des Deutschen Archæologischen Institut.*
Ergänzungsheft XIII.
Berlin 1937.

Johansen 1994
Fl. Johansen, *Katalog. Grækenland i arkaisk tid. Ny Carlsberg Glyptotek.*
Copenhagen 1994.

Jucker 1970
H. Jucker, Etruscan votive bronzes from Populonia, in
Art and Technology, 195-219.

Jucker 1973
H. Jucker, Altes und Neues zur Grächwiler Hydria,
AK 9. Beiheft 1973, 42-61.

Jürgeit 1983
F. Jürgeit, Beobachtungen zu einigen sardischen Gewändern, in *Antidoron, Festschrift Jürgen Thimme.*
Karlsruhe 1983, 119-124.

Karakasi 2001
K. Karakasi, *Archaische Koren,*
Munich 2001.

Karageorghis 1997
V. Karageorghis, Greek Gods and Heroes in Cyprus: a Preview of the Problem, in
Greek Offerings 1997, 221-229.

La formazione della città in Emilia Romagna – prime esperienze urbane attraverso le nuove scoperte archeologiche. Bologna, Museo Civico Archeologico 26/9 1987-24/1 1988 (ed. C. B. Montanari), II, 1987, 303, fig. 206; 304 cat.no. 1a-c.
Bologna 1987/1988.

Lamb 1929
W. Lamb, *Greek and Roman Bronzes.*
London 1929.

Lamb 1968
W. Lamb, *Greek and Roman Bronzes.*
Reprint Chicago 1968.

Langlotz 1927
E. Langlotz, *Frühgriechische Bildhauerschulen.*
Nürnberg 1927.

Langlotz 1939
E. Langlotz in H. Schrader (ed.), *Die archaischen Marmorbildwerke der Akropolis.*
Frankfurt a/M 1939 (2nd ed. 1969).

Langlotz 1975
E. Langlotz, *Studien zur Nordostgriechische Kunst.*
Mainz a/R 1975.

Lebel 1961
P. Lebel, *Catalogue des Collections Archéologigues de Besancon* V. *Les Bronzes figurés.*
I Planches Paris 1959 (*Annales littéraires de l'université de Besancon* 26, Archéologie 8),
II Texte Paris 1961 (*Annales littéraires de l'université de Besancon* 57, Archéologie 15).
Paris 1961.

Lehmann 1946
P. W. Lehmann, *Statues on Coins.*
New York 1946.

Leibundgut 1990
A. Leibundgut, Polykletische Elemente bei Späthellenistischen und Römischen Kleinbronzen, in
Polyklet 1990.
Frankfurt a/M 1990, 397-449.

Lilliu 1966
G. Lilliu, *Scultura della Sardegna Nuragica.*
Cagliari 1966.

Lisippo 1995
P. Moreno (ed.), *Lisippo, L'arte e la fortuna.*
Monza 1996.

Liisberg 1897
H. C. Bering Liisberg, *Kunstkammeret. Dets Stiftelse og Ældste Historie.*
Copenhagen 1897.

von Lorentz 1935
Fr. von Lorentz, Eine Bronzestatuette des Alexanders des Grossen,
RM 50, 1935, 333-338.

Loseri 1965
L. Ruaso Loseri,
Arte e civiltà romana nell'Italia settentrionale dalla repubblica alla Tetrarchia.
Catalogo della Mostra, Bologna 1964.
Bologna 1965.

Maetzke 1957
G. Maetzke, La collezione del Museo Nazionale di Chiusi. Per un Corpus dei bronzetti etruschi,
StEtr XXV, 1957, 489-523.

Maggiani 1991
A. Maggiani, Un nuovo bronzetto da Volterra,
ArCl XLIII, 1991,2, 985-999.

Magi 1934
F. Magi, Due bronzetti archaici del territorio fiesolano,
StEtr VIII, 1934, 413-418.

Magi/Beazley 1939
F. Magi/J. D. Beazley, *La raccolta Benedetto Gugliemi nel Museo Gregoriano Etrusco.*
Vatican 1939.

Maiuri 1926
A. Maiuri, Sepino,
NS 1926, 244-251.

Mansuelli 1946-47
G. A. Mansuelli, Bronzetti inediti del Museo Civico di Bologna,
StEtr XIX, 1946-47, 315-329.

Mattiocco 1973
E. Mattiocco, Il culto di Ercole tra i Peligni,
Quaderni di Abruzzo 8, 1973.
Sulmona 1973.

Mattiocco 1989
E. Mattiocco (ed.), *Dalla villa di Ovidio al santuario di Ercole.*
Sulmona 1989.

Mattiocco/van Wonterghem 1989
E. Mattiocco/F. van Wonterghem, La Fortuna di Ercole tra i Peligni, in
Dalla villa di Ovidio al santuario di Ercole.
Sulmona 1989, 47-70.

Maule 1988
Quentin Maule, The Monteguragazza Style,
StEtr LIV, 1986 (1988), 61-74.

Maule 1992
Quentin Maule, Etrusco-Italian Bronzes: The Todi Workshop,
StEtr LVIII, 1992 (1993), 75-88.

Mazzolai 1958
A. Mazzolai, *La collezione del Museo Archeologico di Grosseto. Per un Corpus dei bronzetti etruschi.*
StEtr XXVI, 1958, 193-223.

Menzel 1960
H. Menzel, *Die römishen Bronzen aus Deutschland* I.
I Speyer.
Mainz a/R 1960.

Menzel 1966
H. Menzel, *Die römischen Bronzen aus Deutschland* II *Trier. Rheinisches Landesmuseum.*
Mainz a/R 1966.

Messerchmidt 1942
Fr. Messerschmidt, Review of P. J. Riis, Tyrrhenika, in
GGA (Göttingische Gelehrte Anzeiger),
204, 1942, 97-105.

Micali 1810
G. Micali, *Antichi Monumenti per servire all'opera intitolata L'Italia avanti il Dominio dei Romani.*
Florence 1810.

Milani 1905
L. A. Milani, Montecalvario. Ipogeo paleo-etrusco di Montecalvario presso Castellina in Chianti.
NS 1905, 225-242.

Milani 1912
L. A. Milani, *Il Reale Museo Archeologico di Firenze.*
Florence 1912.

Mingazzini 1932
P. Mingazzini, Fiesole, edicola e stipe votiva rinvenute nella villa già di proprietà Marchi.
NS 1932, 442-481.

Mitten/Doeringer 1967
D. G. Mitten/S.F. Doeringer, *Master Bronzes From The Classical World.*
Mainz 1967.

Moltesen 1982
M. Moltesen, Membra collecta,
ARID IX, 1982, 27-40.

Moltesen/Nielsen 1996
M. Moltesen/M. Nielsen, *Katalog. Etrurien og Mellemitalien. 450-30 f.Kr. Ny Carlsberg Glyptotek.*
Copenhagen 1996.

Monacchi 1988
D. Monacchi, Nota sulla stipe votiva di Grotta Bella (Terni).
StEtr. 54, 1986 (1988), 75-99.

Monti 1965
P. Monti, Catalogo dei bronzetti etruschi e italici in Romagna, in
Studi Romagnoli XIV, 1965.

Moreno 1995
P. Moreno (ed.), *Lisippo. L'Arte e la fortuna.*
Progetto di Paolo Moreno.
Monza 1995.

Moretti 1964
M. Moretti, *Il Museo Nazionale di Villa Guilia.*
Rome 1964.

Morricone 1933
L. Morricone, *Bronzetti etruschi del Museo Civico di Bologna.*
Rome 1933.

Morricone Matini 1975
M. L. Morricone Matini, *Mosaici antichi in Italia. Regione prima. Antium.*
Rome 1975.

Musei Etrusci quod Gregorius XVI, Pon. Max. in Aedibus Vaticanis constituit Monimenta
Ex Aedibus Vaticanis 1842.
Vatican 1842.

Münzen und Medaillen. Auktion.
Kunstwerke der Antike.
Basel.

Neugebauer 1921
K. A. Neugebauer, *Antike Bronzestatuetten.*
Berlin 1921.

Neugebauer 1936
K. A. Neugebauer, Kohlenbecken aus Clusium und Verwandtes.
RM 51, 1936, 181-211.

Ny Carlsberg Glyptoteket 1907
Billedtavler til Kataloget over antike Kunstværker (BT).
Copenhagen 1907.

Ny Carlsberg Glyptothek 1928
Bildertafeln des Etruskischen Museums (Helbig Museum) der Ny Carlsberg Glyptothek.
Copenhagen 1928.

Ohly 1976
D. Ohly, *Die Aegineten. Band I. Die Ostgiebelgruppe.*
Munich 1976.

Ohly, without year
D. Ohly, *Die Antikensammlungen am Königsplatz in München. Ein Führer durch das Museum.*
5th edition
Munich without year.

Padova Preromana 1976
Padova Preromana Nuovo Museo Civico Agli Eremitani.Padova, 27 giugno-15 novembre 1976.
(edd. G. Fogolari/A.M. Chieco Bianchi et al.).
Padova 1976.

Papi 1989
R. Papi, Le immagini popolari di Ercole, in
Dalla villa di Ovidio al santuario di Ercole.
Sulmona 1989, 71-86.

Papi 1991 (1992)
R. Papi, Testimonianze archeologiche della valle dell'Orte. Il deposito votivo di Caramanico, in
Quaderni di Abruzzo. La valle dell'Orte. Ambiente, Cultura, Società.
Atti del Convegno Caramanico 1991.
Chieti 1992.

Papi 1997
R. Papi, La rappresentazione di Ercole nella produzione votive in bronzo di area sabellica, in
A. Campanelli/A. Faustoferri (edd.),
I luoghi degli dei. Sacro e natura nell'Abruzzo italico, Catalogo della mostra (Chieti 1997), Pescara, 142-147.

Payne/Young 1936
H. Payne/G.M.Young,
Archaic Marble Sculpture from the Acropolis.
London 1936.

Pegasus 1997
Pegasus og Tanagra. Antiken i J. F. Willumsens Kunst og Samling.
Exhibition Catalogue 1997
(edd. L. Krogh/P. Guldager Bilde).
Copenhagen 1997.

Perdrizet 1911.
P. Perdrizet, *Bronzes grecs d'Egypte de la collection Fouquet.*
Paris 1911.

Pietrangeli 1953.
C. Pietrangeli, *Mevania (Italia romana, municipi e colonie, Ser.* I,XIII*).*
Rome 1953.

Pinza 1905
G. Pinza,
MAL XV, 1905, cc. 270 ff.

Polyklet 1990.
Polyklet, Der Bildhauer der Griechischen Klassik.
Ausstellung im Liebighaus
17. 10. 1990 - 20. 1. 1991.
Frankfurt a/M 1990.

Popovic et al. 1969
Lj. B. Popovic, *Anticka Bronza u Jugoslaviji 1844-1969*
(ed. Narodni Musej Beograd)
Belgrade 1969.

Poulsen 1927
F. Poulsen, Aus einer alten Etruskerstadt.
(Kgl. Danske Videnskabernes Selskab hist-fil. Meddelelser. XII).
Copenhagen 1927.

Prima Italia 1981
Prima Italia, L'Arte italica del I millennio a.C.
Exhibition Catalogue. Museo Luigi Pigorini. 18 Marzo - 30 Aprile 1981
Rome 1981.

Reinach
S. Reinach,
Répertoire de la statuaire grecque et romaine,
Paris 1897-1930
I 1897
II 1897
III 1904
IV 1910
V 1924
VI 1930

Richardson 1953
E. H. Richardson, The Etruscan origins of Early Roman Sculpture,
MAAR XXI, 1953, 77-124.

Richardson 1964
E. Richardson, *The Etruscans. Their Art and Civilization.*
Chicago/London 1964.

Richardson 1983
E. Richardson, *Etruscan Votive Bronzes, Geometric, Orientalizing, Archaic,* I-II.
Mainz a/R 1983.

Richter 1915,
G. M. A. Richter, *Greek, Etruscan and Roman Bronzes. The Metropolitan Museum of Art.*
New York 1915.

Richter 1953
G. M. A. Richter, *Handbook of The Greek Collection in the Metropolitan Museum of Art.*
New York 1953.

Richter 1960
G. M. A. Richter, *Kouroi.*
London 1960.

Richter 1965
G. M. A. Richter, *The Portraits of the Greeks* I-III.
London 1965.

Richter 1968
G. M. A. Richter,
Korai. Archaic Greek Maidens.
London 1968.

de Ridder 1913
A. de Ridder, *Les Bronzes antiques du Louvre* I. *Les Figurines.*
Paris 1913.

Riis 1938
P. J. Riis, Some Campanian Types of Heads, in
From The Collections of The Ny Carlsberg Glyptothek II, *1938.*
Copenhagen 1938, 140-168.

Riis 1941
P. J. Riis, *Tyrrhenika.*
Copenhagen 1941.

Riis 1946,
P. J. Riis, The Bronze Statuette From Uffington, Berkshire,
JRS XXXVI, 1946, 43-47.

Riis 1957
P. J. Riis, The Bigger Kore from Rimini.
StEtr XXV, 1957, 31-38.

Riis 1962
P. J. Riis, *Den etruskiske Kunst, 2nd ed.*
Copenhagen 1962.

Riis 1997
P. J. Riis, Vulcentia Vetustiora. A Study of Archaic Vulcian Bronzes. *The Royal Danish Academy of Sciences and Letters, Historisk-filosofiske Skrifter* 19. Copenhagen 1997.

Rimini Divina 2000
(edd. A. Fontemaggi/O. Piolanti), *Rimini Divina. Religione e devozione nell'evo antico.* Rimini, Museo della Città, 28 ottobre 2000-20 maggio 2001. Rimini 2000.

Rolley 1967
C. Rolley, *Monumenta graeca et romana.* Ed. H. F. Mussche, Vol. 5, Greek Minor Arts, Fasc. I, The Bronzes. Leiden 1967.

Rolley 1984
C. Rolley, *Die griechischen Bronzen.* Munich 1984.

Romano 1750
Fr. Valesio Romano/A. Fr. Corio Florentino/ R. Venuti Cortonense *Museum Cortonense in Academia Etrusca.* Roma 1750.

Romagna 1982
La Romagna fra VI e IV secolo a.C., Bologna 1982.

Romualdi 1981
A. Romualdi, *Museo Archeologico Nazionale, Firenze. Catalogo del deposito di Brolio in Val di Chiana.* Rome 1981.

Romualdi 1987
A. Romualdi, Rimini, Covignano; stipe votiva di Villa Ruffi, in *La Formazione della città in Emilia Romagna,* Bologna 1987, 302-304.

RVAp
A. D. Trendall/A. Cambitoglou, *The Red-Figured Vases of Apulia* I, Oxford 1978.

von Sacken 1871
E. von Sacken, *Die antiken Bronzen des K.-K. Münz-und Antiken-Cabinets in Wien.* Vienna 1871.

Salskov Roberts 2000
H. Salskov Roberts, Herakles Holding the Horn of Acheloos. Bronze statuettes in the Danish National Museum, in *"Between Orient and Occident", Studies in Honour of P. J. Riis.* The National Museum of Denmark. Copenhagen 2000, 63-75.

Salskov Roberts 2002
H. Salskov Roberts, Types of Herakles Statuettes in Copenhagen that Reflect Large Classical Sculptures, *JRA Suppl. Series* No. 39, vol.2, 2002.

Samnium 1991
Archeologia del Molise. (edd. S. Capini/A. Di Niro). Rome 1991.

Sannibale 1995
M. Sannibale, Qualche osservazione su una statuetta di Venere orientale del Museo Gregoriano Egizio. *Monumenti, Musei e Gallerie pontificie, Bollettino* XV, 1995, 15-35.

Santuari 1985
Santuari d'Etruria, (ed. G. Colonna) Milan 1985.

Sassatelli 1981
G. Sassatelli, *La piccola plastica in bronzo.* Imola 1981.

Scarpignato 1986
M. Scarpignato, Bronzetti votivi da Bettona. *Annali della Facoltà di Lettere e Filologia dell'Università degli Studi di Perugia,* XXIII, n.s.IX, 1985-86. Perugia 1985-1986.

Schumacher 1890
K. Schumacher, *Sammlung antiker Bronzen.* Karlsruhe 1890.

SNG
Sylloge Nummorum Graecorum. The Royal Collection of Coins and Medals. The Danish National Museum.

Sogliano 1889
A. Sogliano, *Il museo provinciale sannitico di Campobasso.* Napoli 1889

Spadea 1996
R. Spadea, Il tesoro di Hera *Boll d'Arte* 88, 1994, 1-34.

Spengler 1820
J. C. Spengler (1767-1839) (Keeper of the Royal Danish Kunstkammer), Handwritten Notes.

Sprenger 1972
M. Sprenger, *Die etruskische Plastik des V. Jahrhunderts v. Chr. und ihr Verhältnis zur griechischen Kunst.* Rome 1972.

Sprenger/Bartoloni 1977
M. Sprenger/G. Bartoloni, *Die Etrusker.* Munich 1977.

Staccioli 1957
R. A. Staccioli, Un bronzetto di Ercole dal territorio Ferrarese, *ArCl* IX, 1957, 26-43.

Stefani 1935
E. Stefani, Gualdo Tadino. *NS* 1935, 155-173.

Strong 1968
D. Strong, *The Early Etruscans.* London 1968.

Stuart 1990
A. Stuart, *Greek Sculpture* I-II. New Haven/London 1990.

Studi Maetzke 1984
Studi di Antichità in onore di Guglielmo Maetzke I-III. Rome 1984.

Tagliamonte 1994
G. Tagliamonte, *I Figli di Marte.* Tyrrhenica III (ed. G. Colonna). Rome 1994.

Tanagra. Exhibition, Aarhus University, 7. september-20. oktober 1996. (Edd. P. Guldager Bilde/L. Krogh). Aarhus 1996.

Taramelli 1909
A. Taramelli, Serri, Scavi nella città pre-romana sull'altopiano di S. Vittoria, *NS* 1909, 412-423.

Taramelli 1913
A. Taramelli, Dolianova, *NS* 1913, 93-96; Nuragus 96-101.

Terrosi Zanco 1961
O. Terrosi Zanco, Ex-voto allungati dell'Italia Centrale, *StEtr.* 29, 1961, 423-459.

Testa 1989
A. Testa/M. Sannibale, *Candelabri e Thymiateria. Monumenti Musei e Gallerie Pontificie. Museo Gregoriano Etrusco.* Cataloghi, 2. Rome 1989.

Thimme 1980
(ed. J. Thimme), *Kunst und Kultur Sardiniens. Ausstellung Badisches Landesmuseum Karlsruhe 18. April-13. Juli 1980.* Karlsruhe 1980.

Thimme 1983
J. Thimme, *Kunst der Sarden.* Munich 1983.

Thomas 1981
R. Thomas, *Athleten Statuetten der Spätarchaik und des strengen Stils.* (Archeologia 18). Rome 1981.

Torelli 2000
M. Torelli, *The Etruscans.* Exhibition Catalogue, Palazzo Grassi, Venice. Milan 2000.

Torelli 2004
M. Torelli, Quali Greci a Gravisca? *AnnMusFaina* XI, 2004, 119-147.

Trendall/Cambitoglou 1978
A. D. Trendall/A. Cambitoglou, *The Red-Figured Vases of Apulia.* Oxford 1978.

Viacava 1994
A. Viacava, *L'atleta di Fano.* (Studia Archaeologica 74). Rome 1994.

Walters 1899
H. B. Walters, *Catalogue of the Bronzes. Greek, Roman and Etruscan in the Department of Greek and Roman Antiquities. British Museum.* London 1899.

van Wonterghem 1973
F. van Wonterghem, Le culte d'Hercule chez les paeligni, *L'Antiquité Classique* 42, 1973, 36-48.

van Wonterghem 1992
F. van Wonterghem, Il culto di Ercole fra i popoli osco-sabellici, in Héraclès d'une rive à l'autre de la Méditerranée. Bilan et perspectives. *Actes de la table ronde de Rome*, Academia Belgica/École francaise de Rome, 15-16 septembre 1989. Brussels 1992.

Woodford 1976
S. Woodford, Heracles Alexikakos Reviewed, *AJA* 80, 1976, 291-294.

List of inventory numbers

List of inventory numbers

Inv. no. ABa 19. Cat. 115
Inv. no. ABa 44. Cat. 122
Inv. no. ABa 45. Cat. 105
Inv. no. ABa 47. Cat. 86
Inv. no. ABa 48. Cat. 81
Inv. no. ABa 49. Cat. 85
Inv. no. ABa 155. Cat. 17
Inv. no. ABa 158. Cat. 18
Inv. no. ABa 159. Cat. 6
Inv. no. ABa 165. Cat. 59
Inv. no. ABa 167. Cat. 61
Inv. no. ABa 219. Cat. 83
Inv. no. ABa 220. Cat. 91
Inv. no. ABa 221. Cat. 82
Inv. no. ABa 222. Cat. 87
Inv. no. ABa 223. Cat. 84
Inv. no. ABa 224. Cat. 94
Inv. no. ABa 225. Cat. 117
Inv. no. ABa 226. Cat. 95
Inv. no. ABa 227. Cat. 108
Inv. no. ABa 228. Cat. 111
Inv. no. ABa 229. Cat. 118
Inv. no. ABa 230. Cat. 103
Inv. no. ABa 231. Cat. 88
Inv. no. ABa 232. Cat. 104
Inv. no. ABa 234. Cat. 121
Inv. no. ABa 235. Cat. 123
Inv. no. ABa 236. Cat. 90
Inv. no. ABa 243. Cat. 125
Inv. no. ABa 245. Cat. 112
Inv. no. ABa 247. Cat. 74
Inv. no. ABa 263. Cat. 126
Inv. no. ABa 468a. Cat. 21
Inv. no. ABa 468b. Cat. 23
Inv. no. ABa 468c. Cat. 22
Inv. no. ABa 469. Cat. 10
Inv. no. ABa 470a. Cat. 38
Inv. no. ABa 470b. Cat. 36
Inv. no. ABa 470c. Cat. 37
Inv. no. ABa 470d. Cat. 11
Inv. no. ABa 564. Cat. 12
Inv. no. ABa 578. Cat. 69A
Inv. no. ABa 579. Cat. 78
Inv. no. ABa 707. Cat. 42
Inv. no. ABa 781. Cat. 113
Inv. no. ABa 868. Cat. 5
Inv. no. ABa 869. Cat. 51
Inv. no. ABa 874. Cat. 68
Inv. no. 93. Cat. 44
Inv. no. 116. Cat. 54
Inv. no. ABa 234. Cat. 121
Inv. no. 133. Cat. 49
Inv. no. 516. Cat. 9
Inv. no. 615. Cat. 57
Inv. no. 823. Cat. 106
Inv. no. 946. Cat. 55
Inv. no. 1248,1-1248,33. Cat. 29
Inv. no. 1249a-1249n. Cat. 39
Inv. no. 1250a. Cat. 15
Inv. no. 1250b. Cat. 124
Inv. no. 1250c. Cat. 98
Inv. no. 1250d. Cat. 109
Inv. no. 1250e. Cat. 102
Inv. no. 1250f. Cat. 110
Inv. no. 1250g. Cat. 96
Inv. no. 1250h. Cat. 97
Inv. no. 1250i. Cat. 101
Inv. no. 1251c. Cat. 77
Inv. no. 1252. Cat. 50
Inv. no. 1255. Cat. 116
Inv. no.1257a. Cat. 70
Inv. no. 1257b. Cat. 65
Inv. no. 1257c. Cat. 64
Inv. no. 1257d. Cat. 75
Inv. no. 1257e. Cat. 76
Inv. no. 1731. Cat. 53
Inv. no. 1732. Cat. 114
Inv. no. 1734. Cat. 67
Inv. no.1910. Cat. 71
Inv. no. 2289. Cat. 135
Inv. no. 3094. Cat. 129
Inv. no. 3095. Cat. 130
Inv. no. 3242. Cat. 47
Inv. no. 3762. Cat. 89
Inv. no. 3763. Cat. 93
Inv. no. 4198. Cat. 46
Inv. no. 4203. Cat. 56
Inv. no. 4752. Cat. 48
Inv. no. 4787. Cat. 26
Inv. no. 4788. Cat. 28
Inv. no. 4789. Cat. 27
Inv. no. 4790 *2 pieces. Cat. 31
Inv. no. 4791. Cat. 32
Inv. no. 4792. Cat. 34
Inv. no. 4793. Cat. 35
Inv. no. 4794. Cat. 33
Inv. no. 4795. Cat. 40
Inv. no. 4796. Cat. 41
Inv. no. 4797. Cat. 66
Inv. no. 4798. Cat. 62
Inv. no. 4807. Cat. 4
Inv. no. 4808. Cat. 3
Inv. no. 4976. Cat. 58
Inv. no. 4982. Cat. 43
Inv. no. 5361. Cat. 134
Inv. no. 5362. Cat. 63
Inv. no. 5366. Cat. 2
Inv. no. 5367. Cat. 1
Inv. no. 5368. Cat. 60
Inv. no. 5369. Cat. 72
Inv. no. 6578. Cat. 16
Inv. no. 8357. Cat. 24
Inv. no. 8358. Cat. 25
Inv. no. 8359. Cat. 19
Inv. no. 8360. Cat. 20
Inv. no. 9831. Cat. 7
Inv. no. 11350. Cat. 79
Inv. no. 13173. Cat. 8
Inv. no. 13340. Cat. 92
Inv. no. 13341. Cat. 45
Inv. no. 13396. Cat. 100
Inv. no. 13397. Cat. 80
Inv. no. 15173. Cat. 120

GÖSTA ENBOM MONOGRAPHS are published with the support of the "Foundation of Consul General Gösta Enbom".

VOLUME 1
POTTERY IN THE ARCHAEOLOGICAL RECORD: GREECE AND BEYOND
Edited by Mark L. Lawall & John Lund.
Aarhus University Press 2011.

VOLUME 2
RED-FIGURE POTTERY IN ITS ANCIENT SETTING
Edited by Stine Schierup and Bodil Bundgaard Rasmussen.
Aarhus University Press 2012.

VOLUME 3
THE TRANSPORT AMPHORAE AND TRADE OF CYPRUS
Edited by Mark L. Lawall & John Lund.
Aarhus University Press 2013.

VOLUME 4
THE REGIONAL PRODUCTION OF RED-FIGURE POTTERY: GREECE, MAGNA GRAECIA AND ETRURIA
Edited by Stine Schierup & Victoria Sabetai.
Aarhus University Press 2014.

VOLUME 5
A STUDY OF THE CIRCULATION OF CERAMICS IN CYPRUS FROM THE 3RD CENTURY BC TO THE 3RD CENTURY AD
John Lund.
Aarhus University Press 2015.

VOLUME 6
DOCUMENTING ANCIENT RHODES: ARCHAEOLOGICAL EXPEDITIONS AND RHODIAN ANTIQUITIES
Edited by Stine Schierup.
Aarhus University Press 2019.

VOLUME 7
CATALOGUE OF THE SARDINIAN, ETRUSCAN AND ITALIC BRONZE STATUETTES IN THE DANISH NATIONAL MUSEUM
Helle Salskov Roberts.
Aarhus University Press 2021.